COLLEGE SURVIVAL

GREG GOTTESMAN
AND FRIENDS

MACMILLAN • USA

Fourth Edition

Macmillan General Reference
A Simon & Schuster Macmillan Company
1633 Broadway
New York, NY 10019

An Arco Book

MACMILLAN is a registered trademark of Macmillan, Inc.
ARCO is a registered trademark of Prentice-Hall, Inc.

Library of Congress Cataloging-in-Publication Data

Gottesman, Greg.
    College survival / Greg Gottesman and friends. -- 4th ed.
       p.   cm.
    At head of title: ARCO.
    ISBN 0-02-861068-7
    1. College student orientation--United States. 2. College
students--United States--conduct of life. 3. College students--
United States--Time management. I. Title.
LB2343.32.G68 1996
378.1'98--dc20   96-12705
                                                   CIP

Manufactured in the United States of America

10 9 8 7 6 5 4 3 2

CONTENTS

Dedication

To my grandma, who taught me so much

About the Author

Greg Gottesman recently graduated from Stanford University with a degree in Political Science. He presently is studying law and business at Harvard University. He lives in Cambridge with his wife, Shannon. In his free time, Greg enjoys writing, telling stories, and playing tennis.

THE ADVENTURES OF JOE D. ZASTER

Acknowledgments

For this fourth edition of *College Survival*, I have some new friends to thank.

To my new wife Shannon, thank you for being supportive of my work on *College Survival*, in spite of our grueling graduate school schedules.

A special thanks to Dr. Lauren Warshal Cohen, who has taught at community college for the past several decades. Dr. Cohen and several of her students put together the new chapter on community colleges. Their advice and stories add a lot to this edition.

Martina Stewart, a recent graduate of Yale University, helped write the chapter on the minority experience. Her insights and experiences were integral to this important new chapter.

Most of *College Survival* has stayed exactly the same as when I wrote it in my freshman and sophomore years at Stanford University. Once again, let me thank the people who made that first edition possible.

Reliable sources tell me that my mom actually came up with the idea for *College Survival*. Both my parents helped edit the book, especially my mom. My dad was particularly helpful in editing the computer chapter and in adding some corny jokes.

My journalist grandma, Mary K. Brown, to whom the book is dedicated, gave me solid advice during every phase of the book. If I dare call myself a writer, she deserves all the credit. I'm embarrassed to say how many high school English papers she corrected.

My friend, Steve Ojemann, who is now finishing medical school, drew all the wonderful cartoons. Thank you for your wit, Steve.

Chip Shields, a high school counselor and author of *The College Guide to Parents*, deserves much of the credit for helping me get this book published. I also want to thank Linda Bernbach and Christina Buffamonte at ARCO for all their help, patience, and wisdom. Lisa Bianchi, formerly at ARCO, was especially helpful in organizing the first edition.

The heart and soul of this book, however, belongs to the contributors. I especially would like to thank the following students for their extensive work in these areas: Rico Alexander on packing, Rick Arney and Stanley Ryter on banking, Christina Buffamonte on commuting, Bryan Cohen on partying, Matt Crile on Greek versus dorm life, Andy Gottesman on choosing classes and orientation, Leslie Friend on health, nutrition, and Greek versus dorm life, Tara McCann on getting involved, Whitney Morris on what to bring for your dorm room, Thom McDade on time management, Tami Ostroff on clothing, John Pilafidis and Jamie Reynolds on computers, John Schreuder on working at school, David Stern on cars, Keith Vernon on athletics and exercise, Noeleen Walder on campus safety, and Jessica Hall on roommates.

Finally, for answering all my nagging questions, I want to thank Dr. Jeff Tauben, Dr. Nancy Schuette, Ethan Diamond, Maureen Strasser, and Paddy Carson. Alita Kiaer, my favorite English teacher, always deserves special mention. And to the many people at the health clinics, department stores, libraries, laundromats, airlines, packing centers, and service stations, thank you too!

Greg Gottesman

Preface

"In my end is my beginning."

—T.S. ELIOT

For many, getting that fat envelope in the mail is a relief. And why not? A college acceptance letter invariably symbolizes the end of four long years of high school. No more fights with dad over keys to the car. No more arguments with mom about "independence." Indeed, no more worrying about who you are going to spend Homecoming with or who you are going to sit with in the school cafeteria.

But don't let anyone fool you. College is by no means an end to your jaded past; in fact, it is more of a beginning. It is the beginning of learning to be responsible, independent, and street smart. Balancing a checkbook, washing dirty clothes, deciding what to bring to school, making your own airline reservations, choosing between a fraternity and a dormitory, communicating with a roommate about his or her "hygiene habits," interior decorating . . . these are all mountains that each college student will at one time or another attempt to conquer.

This book, written by college kids from all over the country, will not give you all the answers to university life; what it will give you are facts, accurate information, and alternatives. It will tell you how to avoid the woes of a college freshman who was forced to wear dull pink the entire fall quarter. It will give you tips on college dating. It will familiarize you with the wrong and right things to pack up for East, West, and Midwest travel. It will teach you about hundreds of other things every college freshman should know before taking the big plunge.

In all, this book will make you a better, more informed decision-maker. The transition between home and college life is not easy. The purpose of this book is to change that.

The following pages offer an education, not just in a class-room sense, but in a life one as well. As Mark Twain once said, "Don't let school get in the way of your education."

Twain never was a student.

Good luck.

CHAPTER 1

Clothing: What To Bring

> *I love clothes, cosmetics, socks, shoes ...
> heck, I love just about everything you can put
> in a suitcase. No wonder I had problems
> packing for college.*
>
> *After making trips to the back-to-school sale at
> Nordstroms and the local discount drugstore, I
> raced home—the moment of truth had
> arrived. First I made a few neat piles on the
> floor, but soon I abandoned that method and
> started throwing everything into the empty
> bags. Next thing you know, my bags were
> ready to burst, not even enough space for a
> few pairs of underwear.*
>
> *"Wait a second!" I thought to myself. "What in
> the world did I pack? Did I forget socks?"*
>
> *Luckily, you always can empty your bags
> and start again. But it's probably smarter to
> pack in an orderly fashion the first time.*
>
> —TAMI OSTROFF, POMONA COLLEGE

 Psst ... For your convenience, a tear-out checklist with all your packing essentials appears on pages 233-237. Please refer it as you go through Chapters 1 and 2.

THE DON'TS OF PACKING COLLEGE CLOTHING

1. DON'T OVERPACK.

Take what you know you will wear. The stuff you "think" you might wear, you won't!

A few ways to judge if you've overpacked: Can you zip your suitcase? Can you carry the suitcases to the car? Do the front wheels of the car lift off the ground when the trunk is loaded? Is the airline willing to ship your bags with no additional freight charges?

2. DON'T PACK FOR THE BAHAMAS. REMEMBER THE CLIMATE.

Are you going to Tempe, Arizona or Ithaca, New York? Did you take enough Bermuda shorts or heavy sweaters? Did you take too many?

Climate should play a major role in wardrobe decisions.

3. DON'T PACK MOM'S FAVORITES.

Being a last-minute person, I was in a crunch when it came time to pack for college. My mom ended up doing the majority of packing for me. What a mistake!

Instead of packing what I wanted, I ended up with my mom's favorites. I had these wool sweaters, which were about as comfortable as the neck brace from my orthodontist. I had too many nice T-shirts and nothing to play basketball in. When I drove home a few weekends later, I had to do the whole packing thing over again.

—DAN GOTTESMAN, UNIVERSITY OF WASHINGTON

Pack what you will be comfortable wearing. You won't wear mom's favorites once at school.

4. DON'T PACK A LOT OF CLOTHES THAT NEED DRY CLEANING OR
     IRONING.

Ironing is a pain and hand-washing is totally out of the
question.

Consider easy-care fabrics. Although 100% cotton and
100% wool are chic, they require extra care. 60/40 polyester/
cotton does not wrinkle as much.

5. DON'T BE SOMEONE ELSE.

If you have your own style of dress, don't be afraid to show
it. At college, individuality is admired just as much as con-
formity. In fact, nonconformist attire is often trendy on college campuses.

6. DON'T FORGET TO CHECK THE BATHROOM AND BEDROOM
     DRAWERS.

Before leaving, take a walk around your bedroom and bathroom. If you see any drawers still unopened, you probably
have forgotten something. Check again.

Underwear, Socks, Pajamas, etc.

Underwear is always the first thing you run out of. Bring
lots. Socks, too! You don't want to be doing a wash every five
days.

A big bathrobe, especially for women, may be a lifesaver on
coed floors. The walk from the shower to your room may be
quite a hike.

Casual Wear

Of course, what you bring should depend foremost on your personality and on the climate in which you will be living.

But blue jeans, T-shirts, and sweatshirts receive extra "thumbs up" because of their versatility. In addition, it's hard to beat sweats and a baseball cap when you are late for a 9 A.M. class.

Remember light (e.g., white) clothes will keep you cooler in hot climates as they will repel the sun's heat.

Bathroom Buddies: Towels and Cosmetics

> *It seemed at least half my graduation gifts were not checks or pens but towels. I began wondering whether my friends thought I was dirty or needed to shower more often. In any case, I took nearly all the towels to school with me. They turned out to be a great graduation gift.*
>
> —Whitney Morris, Pomona College

You will want at least three or four big bath towels and maybe another for sunbathing and one or two washcloths.

Cosmetics are pretty self-explanatory. Bring what you need.

Shoes

Shoes hog suitcase space. Take only what you will wear. You won't have room to be Imelda Marcos. Also, remember the climate in which you will be residing: Sandals are more practical in California than in North Dakota.

JEWELRY

Be especially careful with your valuable jewelry. Don't bring a diamond Rolex unless you are feeling charitable. Remember that your roommate might not be as careful at locking the doors as you are.

FORMAL WEAR

You are going to need some nice-looking duds for job interviews, religious services, and/or formals, but not necessarily a tuxedo or the like.

If you don't have a tuxedo and one is required, rent one. Later, after you see how many times you need a tuxedo, you might find it more cost efficient to buy one. For the most part, though, formal collegiate gatherings require a sports

> *I only brought one of my fancy dresses to college. Girls who bring more are just asking for trouble. First of all, you always are going to have problems with storage, especially in sororities. Chances are, your dress will be mushed in between all your other stuff. Besides, if you are ever in a crunch, you can always borrow a dress from a friend. They usually don't mind as long as you return the favor.*
>
> —STEPHANIE SLEIGHT, OREGON STATE UNIVERSITY

jacket—nothing more! A navy blue blazer and gray slacks are usually a sure bet on any campus.

Women should have at least one formal dress at college. If you don't like to wear dresses more than a few times, trading with friends is more than acceptable.

OUTERWEAR FOR COLDER CLIMATES

"Don't be stuck in a Chicago winter without a good pair of gloves," warns Leslie Friend, a senior at the University of Chicago.

Gloves are not the only thing you will need, particularly if you like to ski or plan on attending school in a colder climate. Consult the tear-out checklist.

MEDICAL SUPPLIES

A well-stocked health kit can save you a trip to the infirmary. Since storage space may be limited, determine which items are most necessary.

You can pick up an "Emergency Supply Kit" from the American Red Cross for roughly $20.

SPORTS GEAR

Depending on your sport, you may need certain gear (e.g., squash racket, snorkel gear, or golf clubs). Plan on bringing a few of the basics. For example, you might want a mitt for the inevitable dorm softball game or a tennis racket in case there's a court down the street.

CHAPTER 2

Your Room: What To Bring

When I packed for college last fall, I filled an entire U-Haul trailer with loads of junk that for one reason or another I was convinced I would need. I was sending tons of clothing, extra ski equipment, a teapot, a spare flashlight . . . to name a few.

Needless to say, end-of-the-year packing was sheer misery. I was still at it when my parents arrived to escort me home. I thought I would never leave Pomona. The moral of the story: Take less rather than more. It's amazing all the things you really don't need.

—WHITNEY MORRIS, POMONA COLLEGE

TAKE LESS RATHER THAN MORE!

This chapter should help transform your dormitory room into your castle. Keep three things in mind:

1. You are going to be living there for one year, not a lifetime. College rooms are smaller than you think.

2. Check with your future roommate. Two radios are too many. Two televisions are too many. So are two phones. Avoid duplication.

3. Unless you are going to school in the boonies, a store with everything you could ever need is bound to be around the corner. Don't worry!

BED BASICS

You should consider a washable spread as your bed will become a couch, a study lounge, and a footrest to all who enter.

Check with your school to determine whether the beds are *regular length* or *extra-long*. Regular-sized flat sheets can be used on an extra-long mattress, but fitted sheets must be purchased in the extra-long size.

Check to see if your school has a linen or laundry service. Some schools even provide students with clean sheets and towels each week.

If you have room to store it, bring a sleeping bag. You may want to camp in the surrounding woodland or lend the bag to a visiting friend.

YOUR ACADEMIC HEADQUARTERS: SCHOOL SUPPLIES

Pens and pencils like to get up and walk away; a storage bin will keep them at bay.

You will need a backpack, preferably a large bag, to carry all your junk to class.

BOOKS

You will be buying a whole slew of textbooks at school, but there are a few essential reference books you can bring from home.

☐ A respected dictionary
Suggestion: *American Heritage* or *Webster's New World*

☐ A foreign-language dictionary, if you plan to study a
language
☐ A thesaurus or synonym-finder, preferably in easy-
to-use dictionary form
Suggestion: *Roget's International Thesaurus*
☐ A bible, not necessarily for religious purposes
☐ A book on the rules of English grammar
Suggestion: *The Elements of Style* by William
Strunk, Jr. and E.B. White
☐ A book of quotations
Suggestion: *Bartlett's Book of Quotations*

Lighting

Mom was right. Reading in the dark does strain your eyes
and may trigger headaches. So, if you plan to study, don't be
lazy: Get out of bed and turn on the light.

Large floor lamps take up too much space. Get a good reading lamp for your bed or desk.

Computers and Typewriters

Don't bring both!

If you have your own computer, make sure to take it with
you or ship it. Otherwise, most schools provide extensive
computer facilities as well as reduced rates to students
wishing to buy their own system. (See Chapter 11, Computers.)

Beware of requests to borrow the "machine." You may never
get to use it yourself. Establish a "lending policy" early.

MAKING EXTRA SPACE: STORAGE, CLOSETS AND ORGANIZATION

Two beds can barely fit into some of the rooms at Stanford, let alone two people. So, instead of living like sardines, I decided to do something about it and built a loft.

With the loft in place, my roommate and I had loads of space. We had room for the stereo, a futon, plants, more shelves . . . more everything. With just a few pieces of wood and a power saw, I turned our once humble shanty into a palace, of sorts.

—ALEX BERZINS, STANFORD UNIVERSITY

You will not have much space, so be creative when organizing and planning ahead.

A large trunk serves various functions; it can act as a large suitcase, a table, or a base for stacking other storage units.

Baskets perform an assortment of roles as well: shelves, drawers, cupboards, shoe holders, to name a few. Crates work equally well.

If you do not have some already, bookshelves conserve oodles of space. Check your room first. The school may have installed plenty already.

If space is really a problem, you can always build a loft and get rid of one of the beds. Former students are usually in the business of selling their old lofts. For around $50, it may be a good investment, especially if you don't feel like (or can't) build your own.

Curing the Munchies

> *During my freshman year, my roommate and I managed to lure half of the water polo team into our room with the scent of popcorn. An encouraging beginning, we employed the popper frequently, but never again with such success.*
>
> —ERIN CHARLES, UC-BERKELEY

Check with your dormitory, fraternity, or sorority before purchasing any appliances. Many dorms have kitchens with refrigerators, ovens, and microwaves for student use. Also, coordinate with your roommate—no need for two toaster ovens. A refrigerator, hotpot, cups, and kitchen utensils are especially recommended—if they are not provided by the school.

The Dilemma With Refrigerators: To Rent or Buy?

Nearly every college in the Western Hemisphere has commissioned a local organization to rent refrigerators on a semester or yearly basis. The company generally offers the square 1.6 cubic foot size as well as the larger rectangular 2.8 cubic-foot size. Costs vary but $50-$75 dollars is standard. Split between two or three people, the fee becomes more manageable.

Buying a new refrigerator at Sears or a local discount appliance store will run around $100-$150. Over the long haul, this is the more reasonable investment, but you must deal with summer storage and come up with the initial expense. You also must provide your own maintenance.

Renting the first year and then purchasing a used fridge from a graduating senior may be your best bet.

FIVE QUICK TIPS FOR DECORATING YOUR CASTLE

The most memorable room I saw during my freshman year belonged to an unlikely pair of roommates, Brenda and Aileen. Although they had different tastes in almost every area, they managed to coordinate their styles and create a lively environment in a tiny space.

They bought some tacky dime store beads, which hung in strings in the doorway. In the place of honor on the fridge sat a lava lamp named Sybil. Posters of Billy Idol's leering grin were interspersed with posters of The Cure and Monet prints.

Even the ceiling had a special touch. A student who was an astronomy major had lived in the room several years earlier and had positioned glow-in-the-dark stars all over the ceiling. You could lie on the floor and look at actual constellations.

Many a social gathering took place in their humble abode, partly because of the women and partly because of the environment they had created.

—WHITNEY MORRIS, POMONA COLLEGE

DON'T EXPECT PARADISE

Upon arrival, don't entertain delusions of your new room looking like Trump Palace. The Gobi desert would be more apropos.

But all is not lost. A few decorating tips, a few inspired ideas, a few nails, and who knows? . . . *Better Homes and Gardens* beware!

1. POSTERS AND PICTURES ADD PIZAZZ TO ANY WALL.

Posters are easy to find, easy to put up, and even easier on the pocketbook.

Hometown favorites, from a county fair or your city's skyline, attach a local flavor to the room. University stores have huge assortments. Monet prints are especially popular.

Pictures of family and friends can do more than cure hometown blues. They can add life to a wall, a dresser, or a desk.

2. A BULLETIN BOARD IS NEVER TACK-Y.

Along with helping you organize, bulletin boards provide a perfect medium for placing photos you have taken during the year. A bulletin board also means you don't have to bombard your walls with numerous large nails.

 Psst . . . Many schools have rules that disallow the use of nails or pins in walls. Find out about your school's policy before you pick up a hammer. Move cautiously as fines are often steep.

3. THROW-RUGS BEAT ANY DORMITORY FLOOR.

Although expensive, a rug can change the atmosphere of a room. Besides giving a cozy look, a rug provides actual warmth; it keeps the room and your toes comfortable.

Check with graduating seniors and local carpet stores for the best deals.

4. DRESS UP YOUR WINDOWS.

Most dormitory windows come with some sort of covering. If not, you can make your own or buy inexpensive curtains or shades from variety stores. Budding artists have a field day with window treatments, all the way from laminated shades to bamboo rollers.

5. DECORATE THE DOOR.

The quintessential door reflects the personality of those behind it. Crossed-out pictures of ex-boyfriends, rejection letters from rival universities, applications to greasy fast-food chains, articles about the World Wrestling Federation, parking tickets . . . put it all up!

> *This guy down the hall decorated his door with every article he could find relating to the reincarnation of Elvis Presley. I couldn't believe how much he found . . . definitely one of the funniest things I have ever seen.*
>
> —GREG GOTTESMAN, STANFORD UNIVERSITY

You will need some writing apparatus near your door that allows others to leave messages. A note pad with a pencil on a string works well.

For a few more pennies (around $20 worth), you can splurge on an erasable message board.

Psst . . . Remember who's living in the room and who's supposed to enjoy it. Beauty is in the eye of the beholder. But beware . . . decorations such as bare-all centerfolds may offend more people than they impress.

CHAPTER 3

Packing and Sending

> *It was the day before my flight, so I was forced into a packing frenzy. I placed my stereo in a box of clothes and taped the box shut. I then preceded to—get this!—throw the box around the room. I figured if the box could withstand my punishment it certainly could weather whatever the airlines were about to dish out. What in the world was I thinking?*
>
> *When I opened the box, my stereo didn't work. How could it when it was in 100 pieces?*
>
> —RICO ALEXANDER, STANFORD UNIVERSITY

BOXES, BOXES, BOXES . . . START IN THE ATTIC

For those who have never been in their attic, now is a good time. Skip over dad's old prom pictures and the broken transistor radios. You're looking for something else: cardboard boxes. Big boxes. Small boxes. Any and all boxes.

If the attic leaves you empty-handed, try the back alley of a warehouse or ask in a grocery store.

If you want to bypass the search altogether, purchase boxes from a packaging or moving company. Bicycle boxes can be picked up at bike shops or department stores for a minimal charge.

THE SCOOP ON DELIVERY SERVICE: RULES FOR POTENTIAL PACKERS

The procedure for using a delivery service (e.g., United Parcel Service, Federal Express, DHL, and Emery) is pretty standard: Call the service, give them the address where you want the package delivered, state the date you want it there, and estimate the weight of the packages involved. Then, pack your box and drop it at the local carrier. If cumbersome, the deliverer can pick up the goods at your house.

UPS provides a more complete set of guidelines, but these hints should take care of any "physical" packing problems.

1. Use cardboard boxes or a foot locker.

2. Protect items inside with crumpled grocery bags or special packing material (e.g., bubble wrap).

3. Place fragile items toward the middle of the box. The sides are more dangerous.

4. Close your boxes with tape two inches or greater in width. UPS recommends pressure-sensitive plastic or water-activated paper tape, but disapproves of string or rope.

5. Make sure to label the contents of your boxes. This way you can unpack in a systematic fashion.

 Psst . . . If you are sending your worldly goods via a delivery service, set aside sufficient cosmetics, a few wardrobe changes, and a set of sheets and towels. You will want to keep these items with you because belongings don't always arrive as planned.

PACKING TIPS FOR DRIVERS

Driving to school is difficult enough without having to worry about the packing element. Follow these rules:

1. MAKE SURE THERE'S ENOUGH ROOM.

Don't be decapitated by the ski pole that couldn't fit in the back seat. Make sure your car has the space.

Laws forbid the obstruction of a driver's view with excess baggage. Keep the stuff in the back seat as low as possible. When renting a car, ask for the largest size available. The difference in rates is minimal. Count family members as extra baggage. A grandma and two sisters equals about four large boxes.

2. IF SIZE IS A PROBLEM, RENT A U-HAUL TRAILER.

U-Haul trailers can turn small cars with no trunk space into all-purpose trucks, capable of lugging all your belongings to school.

Rates vary depending upon distance, time, and size of trailer. Mark, a manager of a U-Haul center, suggests a 4 × 8 trailer because it is more aerodynamic than the other sizes and therefore more fuel-efficient. A trip from Seattle to Chicago will run approximately $150 and enable you to use the 4 × 8 trailer for nine days.

For a nominal fee, U-Haul will rent you trailer hitches, furniture pads, boxes, and protective locks.

3. GUARD AGAINST THEFT.

Roll up the windows, bring the stuff into the motel room and lock the doors—always. Thieves laugh at cross-country travelers who leave luggage in plain view overnight.

TIPS ON PACKING FOR PLANES AND BUSES

If you are traveling by plane or train, remember to:

1. FIND OUT THE RATES FOR EXTRA BAGGAGE.

Most airlines allow you to check three bags and carry one on board. The charge for each additional bag (or bicycle) is roughly $20.

Greyhound bus service allows two bags on-board and charges $10 for each additional bag. Bus companies may impose a five-bag maximum.

2. WATCH FOR WEIGHT LIMITS.

Greyhound has a 50-pound weight limit, while most airlines have 70-pound limits. If your boxes exceed the limit, look into delivery services.

3. CALL THE AIRLINE OR BUS COMPANY WITH SPECIAL CIRCUMSTANCES.

Some airlines and bus companies have special require-ments with regard to packing certain items. For example, many airlines require you to use their special bicycle boxes, while others ask that you obtain your own. In these cases, calling the airline or bus company is your best bet.

CHAPTER 4

Planes: Flying the Collegiate Skies

I felt kind of guilty making my parents pay for my round-trip ticket home over Winter Break. "I am a college man now," I thought. It was one of those ego trips.

Anyway, when the flight attendant announced that the plane might be overbooked, I dashed over to the counter to let her know that I was willing to give up my seat—for a free round-trip ticket, of course.

To make a short story shorter, I was booted off the flight and received a free round-trip ticket. The kicker was, the airline put me on another flight only 20 minutes later. My parents didn't even know I had been bumped. Even better, I had a great holiday present for my mom when she arrived at the airport—a free round-trip ticket.

—EVERETT HSU, JOHNS HOPKINS UNIVERSITY

EIGHT TIPS FOR CHEAP, SMART PLANE TRAVEL

Before acing your first college final, before marching for liberal causes, before joining a sorority, before doing anything for that matter, you have got to get there.

For those not within driving distance, the "getting there" facet of college life poses maj(air) problems. Maybe you have not flown much or maybe never at all. Maybe you do not know how to find the cheapest flights. Fear not! These next

few hints should make "getting there" (through the air) as simple as one, two, three, four, five, six, seven, and eight.

EIGHT TIPS ON PLANE TRAVEL

1. GET A TRAVEL AGENT OR USE YOUR PARENTS' AGENT.

> *For Spring Break, my roommates and I wanted to go on a cruise. Instead of doing all the work ourselves, we called a travel agent near campus. Not only were his services free, he made all the reservations and saved us loads of time. He also found us the best rates—something I'm not sure I could have done.*
>
> *Even though my mom makes most of my plane reservations with our travel agent at home, I now know how easy it is to use one myself. It sure beats making all the arrangements yourself.*
>
> —JOELLEN TAPPER, OCCIDENTAL COLLEGE

Travel agents can save you hundreds of dollars and hours of time. Better yet, many of them do not charge a penny, making all their commission from the airlines. Ask the travel agent if he or she charges a fee for service.

Since the deregulation of the airline industry, all carriers have been forced to compete for business. Standard fares do not exist today as they once did. In fact, Paul, a travel agent, explained that United Airlines offers 17—count 'em, 17!— different airfares between Seattle and New York alone, depending upon when you purchase the ticket, if the fare is non-refundable, what time you travel, what day of the week, if you are staying over a Saturday night, and which class you choose to fly.

Unless you do hours of research or employ a travel agent, finding the best fare from destination to destination is nearly impossible.

If you still don't believe it, consider that, at the time of printing this book, United charged as much as $463 for a one-way ticket from Seattle to New York, while a round-trip ticket could be had for as little as $198.

Be smart. Get a travel agent. Besides, you can't beat the price.

2. BOOK THE INITIAL PLANE RESERVATION WITH A MAY OR JUNE RETURN.

The problem with plane reservations is that, when you make your initial jaunt to the campus, you probably will not know when your first finals will be completed. Final exams usually last a week; you might finish them in the first two days or have a final on the very last day. In addition, you may not know if you will be coming home for Thanksgiving break. Needless to say, a lot of things are "iffy."

The problem with "iffy" is that the airlines couldn't care less about your scheduling problems. The cheapest fares are nonrefundable and designed for those who know the exact date of their arrival and departure.

Therefore, you should book the return flight of your first round-trip ticket for the last day of finals at the end of the school year in May or June. All other reservations can be made when you are more in control of your plans. Even if you finish your finals early in May or June, you can spend the last days of your freshman year packing and/or partying.

3. ALWAYS MAKE YOUR RETURN RESERVATION FOR THE LATEST POSSIBLE DATE.

As previously mentioned, you may have trouble finding out when your finals are over. If you discover you are able to leave earlier than expected and possess a ticket with a future date, go on standby and try to grab a vacant seat. Although the rules on most tickets say you cannot employ this tactic, an airline's policy seems to be at the discretion of the gate agent. A kind one may take pity and let you on the flight.

However, no gate agent will let you go standby if the date on your return ticket has come and gone. Thus, make your return reservation for the latest possible date. Worse comes to worse, you stay an extra day or two.

4. SIGN UP FOR FREQUENT-FLIER PROGRAMS.

> *Traveling from Seattle to Williamstown, it makes real sense to use the frequent-flier programs. When you are traveling that far and paying that much for tickets, you have to do everything possible to defray the cost. Using the frequent-flier programs is the simplest way to make the airlines work for you.*
>
> —GREG HART, WILLIAMS COLLEGE

Most airlines have frequent-flier programs to encourage you to use the same carrier each time you fly. After flying a certain number of miles, you earn a free flight. Sign up with every airline you use.

Be certain to give your travel agent a mileage number when you book the reservation. Check again at the gate to make sure the mileage number has been entered into the computer.

Many airlines have joined forces with bank credit cards such as VISA and MasterCard, offering frequent flier miles for money charged to specific credit cards. The carriers have teamed with car rental agencies and hotels as well.

Airlines have different mileage requirements to qualify for free trips and/or upgrades. Many airlines work in conjunction with each other. For example, you can use Alaska miles on Horizon, Northwest, or SAS.

5. CHARGE YOUR AIRLINE TICKETS TO YOUR BANK CARD.

What difference does it make how you pay for your ticket? Right? Wrong.

Many bank cards give automatic insurance against lost luggage. Those who have lost suitcases realize the significance of this type of insurance. You have a small fortune locked up in those bags. Be shrewd and, if possible, charge your ticket to a bank card.

By the way, don't send your valuable jewelry or irreplaceable computer disks in the suitcases. Carry valuables on board.

 Psst . . . If your luggage has been damaged on the flight, the airline is responsible. Make sure the airline takes care of all repairs.

6. OFFER TO BE BUMPED AND EARN A FREE ROUND-TRIP TICKET.

As a happy-go-lucky college student, it is often wise to give up your seat if the plane is oversold. Not only do you keep your primary ticket, but you also receive a free round-trip ticket. Free tickets have fewer restrictions and allow ticket holders to change arrival and departure dates without penalty. Open-return tickets like this are a godsend for students with unknown finals schedules.

If you are going to give up your seat, plan on waiting anywhere from 30 minutes to a full day. The airlines will feed you while you are waiting and even pay for a hotel room overnight, if the need arises. Carriers regularly oversell their flights, especially during holidays.

7. WATCH NEWSPAPERS FOR SPECIAL FARES.

When airlines open new routes, they often offer special low fares as incentives. Financially troubled airlines use special rates to lure business. Sometimes the competition follows suit and extends similar fares. Check the newspapers for these special bargains.

Try to be on top of these special prices and book early. Most of the time, an airline will not sell all the seats at a special rate. If you want to be among the lucky ones, don't wait for your travel agent to give you the scoop. He or she may be busy with other clients. Book it yourself.

8. DON'T LOSE YOUR TICKET.

Put the return portion of your ticket in a safe place once you arrive on campus. If you lose your ticket, the airlines will ask you to fill out a lost-ticket application and charge you $50—a rather hefty fee—to process the form. The airlines will then make you pay the full price for another ticket. If it is found that your lost ticket was not used by another person, the airlines will refund the price of the ticket but not the $50.

Those holding "free" tickets (e.g., tickets earned through the frequent-flier programs) need to be especially careful. If you lose one of these, the airline will not refund you a penny, and you will need to purchase an entirely new ticket.

 Psst . . . The best way to keep your airline ticket is to think of it as cash. You wouldn't crumple up a $50 bill and throw it under a pile of garbage. You wouldn't leave a Ben Franklin lying unattended on your dorm room floor. You would put the money in a safe place for later use. Treat your ticket with similar care.

CHAPTER 5

Cars: Driving To and Around Campus

> *I was driving back to Pomona with my girl-friend to start winter quarter. We thought the car was in good shape, so we just took off without checking the transmission fluid or getting oil or any of that stuff.*
>
> *Halfway through the trip, she wakes me up and says, "David, I think the car sounds funny." Of course, we are now in the middle of some mountain pass in the boonies of Northern California.*
>
> *We pulled in at the nearest local service station. Here I am, looking like I just walked out of an L.L. Bean catalogue, totally at the mercy of some local mechanic who probably hadn't had any major business since World War II.*
>
> *I'm sure we ended up paying twice what it cost for transmission fluid and an oil change. Needless to say, I now check my car completely before taking a long journey.*
>
> —DAVID MUSCATEL, POMONA COLLEGE

IS YOUR CAR GOING TO MAKE IT?

If you are driving to school, be realistic about the condition of your car. Don't play "Russian Roulette" with a loaded vehicle.

For students whose school is visible from their bedroom, little car preparation is needed, assuming the car runs adequately.

If your school is more than one state away (or on the other side of Texas), make sure your automobile is ready for the journey. The following should be in order:

☐ All electrical devices in working order
☐ Charged battery
☐ Correctly pressured tires and a spare
☐ First-aid equipment
☐ Flares
☐ Functional windshield-wiper blades
☐ Sufficient windshield-wiper fluid
☐ Jack
☐ Jumper cables
☐ New oil and filter
☐ Sufficient radiator fluid
☐ Sufficient brake fluid
☐ Tool kit

Instead of trying to check all the important fluids yourself, many recommend taking the car into a Jiffy Lube or a similar car-maintenance establishment. These shops will check and change your oil, filter, transmission fluid, brake fluid, windshield-wiper wash, radiator fluid, water, and differential fluid.

Regardless of whether you do it yourself or have it done professionally, you should change your oil about every 5,000 miles.

 Psst . . . It is definitely a good idea to get all the problems with your car taken care of before leaving for college. If your brakes are faulty or your taillight is broken, bring your car to a shop in your hometown. Car problems are the last thing you will want to worry about once at college.

JOINING A MOTOR CLUB AND PLANNING A ROUTE

For long journeys, consult a motor club for a route plan. Although smaller motor companies like Amoco, Shell Motor Club, and Allstate Motor Club offer similar services, the American Automobile Association (AAA) is the largest and most extensive. If you are not a member of one of these clubs, consider joining before venturing to school.

Members of AAA receive Triptiks, maps, tourbooks and travelers checks—free of charge. A Triptik is a comprehensive, day-by-day guide of how to get where you are going. You can prepare a Triptik with an AAA employee a week before your journey.

More importantly, if your car gets stuck on the way, motor clubs come at the ring of a telephone and tow you to safety. For no charge, AAA will travel 10 miles to pick you up. After 10 miles, you pay a slight towing fee, but that's better than being at the mercy of an independent towing company who wants cash and lots of it.

Don't take a chance, especially if you're going to be driving long distances . . . join a club.

SOME DON'TS OF DRIVING YOUR CAR TO SCHOOL

1. DON'T DRIVE ALONE.

Unless you have a short drive, don't risk driving alone. Another person can keep you company—and awake at the wheel.

2. DON'T DRIVE AT NIGHT.

Nighttime means different things to different people. To long-distance drivers, it signifies more accidents. Follow the

8 A.M. to 8 P.M. rule recommended by AAA. Twelve hours of driving is plenty!

3. DON'T WAIT UNTIL THE "NIGHT OF" TO CALL A MOTEL.

If possible, make reservations at a motel the day before you arrive in a city. Driving around unknown city streets looking for accommodations is not productive. Many towns will not have motels with available rooms.

4. DON'T CARRY TOO MUCH CASH.

Cash may be king, but you are a joker if you carry too much. Travelers checks and credit cards are safer.

5. DON'T LEAVE ANYTHING VALUABLE IN YOUR CAR.

Holy Toledo! Don't fall to the same fate as the protagonist in the story on the next page. He left his clothes in the back seat of his car. If you want to keep it, lock your stuff in the trunk or take it with you wherever you go.

6. DON'T DRIVE IN INCLEMENT WEATHER.

If you are driving on the West Coast, this might not be a problem. Otherwise, be careful when Mother Nature starts playing hardball.

During heavy showers, sleet, or snow, pull over and wait it out. Don't ask for trouble. As University of Washington sophomore Skip Slavin warns, "Smaller cars tend to hydroplane in four inches of Pacific Northwest rain."

> *It was the first leg of my journey home from Cornell. Toledo, Ohio was our first overnight stop. We checked in and brought our valuables into the room—stereo, tapes and compact discs.*
>
> *Yet, for some reason, Mr. Justification, that awful demon inside my head, convinced me that I could leave my large blue duffel bag with all my wardrobe in the back seat of the car. I am a short boy—a short, stocky boy. "Who would want my clothes? Who would wear my clothes?" I thought.*
>
> *Obviously, there must be some short, stocky derelict running around out there because the next morning my blue duffel bag was gone. From now on, I don't leave anything in the car.*
>
> —DAVID STERN, CORNELL UNIVERSITY

7. DON'T SPEED . . . BIG BROTHER IN BLACK AND WHITE IS WATCHING!

The speed limit on most interstate highways has been raised to 65. Hopefully, that's high enough to keep most of you closet race car drivers happy.

If you drive over 75 for any length of time, plan on being stopped. Interstates are laden with "fuzz." Besides, you don't want to start off your college career with a speeding ticket.

 Psst . . . Speeding tickets play havoc with your insurance rates, which are probably high enough already.

TIPS AFTER ARRIVAL

You made it to school. Your car is intact. Great! Or is it? Having a car on campus can be a nightmare.

> *However pathetic it sounds, the day mom told me I could take her car to school was one of the happiest moments of my life. Now I could drive for late-night munchies whenever I wanted. I could go to the city on weekends. I could impress women with my rough-and-tumble, four-door Toyota Camry—I wish?*
>
> *I was psyched. That is, I was psyched until the car's transmission blew. Nirvana became hell in a hurry. After calling home several hundred times, visiting 20 some odd transmission dealers, and wasting approximately four full days trying to find the best deal, I was forced to shell out $2,800 to Mr. Aamco for a new transmission. Two days later, my muffler broke. But that's another story.*
>
> *I'm not saying having a car at school isn't great. But sometimes it can be more trouble than it's worth.*
>
> —GREG GOTTESMAN, STANFORD UNIVERSITY

1. HAVE A SET OF JUMPER CABLES HANDY AT ALL TIMES.

Leaving your car in cold weather and forgetting to turn off your lights sap juice from a battery. Jumper cables can save you from sure disaster.

If you are located in an especially cold region, start your car every day and let it run a few minutes. Five or six days of dormancy kills a battery, especially in cold weather.

2. BE CAREFUL WHERE YOU PARK AT SCHOOL.

Meter maids can be nasty on college campuses. Most schools allow you to buy parking passes for campus lots. Often the fee is high, but the cost of several parking tickets is higher.

Parking on streets is usually impossible, unless you are blessed with incredible luck.

> *Parking at the University of Washington is a joke. I literally would skip appointments and not go places just to keep a good spot. It sounds ludicrous but, when you spend an hour and a half one night looking for an opening, you start to cherish a good parking space.*
>
> *I remember my mom asking me if I wanted to drive home for a home-cooked meal once and telling her, "Mom, I know this sounds incredibly stupid, but, if I come home, I am going to lose my parking spot in front of the frat house." It got so bad that I just started keeping my car at home.*
>
> —DAN GOTTESMAN, UNIVERSITY OF WASHINGTON

3. SET A POLICY EARLY ON CAR-SHARING.

If you have a car on campus, friends will wish to borrow it. Set some guidelines early so you don't run into problems.

Many a friend has wrecked a car, and it's your insurance that pays. Expect a gigantic insurance hike or cancellation if your car is involved in an accident with or without you in it. When at all possible, drive your friends where they need to go, instead of just dishing out the keys.

> *I let my roommate borrow my car. It was one of those things where her car broke down at the last minute, so I felt kind of bad for her. The next thing I know, I get a call from the police telling me my car is completely totaled. My roommate was fine, but, after the accident, she never offered to buy me a new car or even a fender. Now, the only thing I can use my car for is used parts. Next time I will definitely think twice about lending out my car so easily.*
>
> —CYNTHIA TWISS, WASHINGTON STATE UNIVERSITY

4. LOCK YOUR DOORS AND TAKE YOUR RADIO INSIDE.

Don't get too attached to that expensive radio in the car. Thousands get stolen each year. If you have a removable car stereo, don't put it in the trunk; that's the first place crooks look. Store it in your room.

Remember thieves thrive on college campuses. Play it safe and always lock your car doors.

DO YOU REALLY NEED A CAR?

Before you drive to school, you must ask yourself: Do I need a car?

Remember that, at most schools, you cannot drive to class; there is either no parking or the classrooms are situated where there are no roads.

Rising insurance rates, having the responsibility of being a chauffeur, being constantly pestered by friends who want to borrow your car, parking, and maintaining the health of your four-wheeler are all problems automobile owners must consider.

So, while a car may provide benefits such as enabling you to drive for late-night snacks and allowing you to leave campus, there are definite drawbacks to having a car as well.

Most people want a car when they go to college. After driving in high school, they're accustomed to the freedom and independence of being able to drive. But I didn't really think I needed a car when I went to college. The hassle of people asking me to borrow it, parking, gas money, repairs, insurance . . . I just thought college would give me enough to worry about.

Also, late-night Denny's stops can become costly, but having to ride your bike to the Denny's off campus will dissuade even a Grand Slam breakfast fanatic from going too often. Of course, this is not to mention the fact that my parents said I absolutely, positively could not have a car.

After my first few quarters, I have decided that I really don't need one. If I am in dire need, I can always find a ride. Plus, college has everything I need right on campus— books, toothpaste, hospital, women.

—JOSEPH ELFORD, STANFORD UNIVERSITY

CHAPTER 6

Orientation

My plane was scheduled to leave for Detroit Metro Airport from Newark at about 4 P.M. I was on my way to a three-day summer orientation program at the University of Michigan in Ann Arbor.

Unfortunately, complications arose as soon as I walked up to the gate to receive a seat assignment. The woman at the terminal told me—get this!—"The runways are too hot, so we will have to cancel flight 293."

"The runways are too hot?" I thought. "You have got to be kidding me."

Luckily, I met these two girls who happened to be going to orientation as well. We talked for about an hour and found out we had some common acquaintances. When we finally got on a plane to Detroit, the pilot gave us some more bad news. "Due to bad weather in Detroit, we've been diverted to Cleveland."

"Cleveland!" we all said in disbelief. "This is getting ridiculous."

By the time we got to Michigan, it was 5 A.M. Orientation was to begin in three hours.

Even though I probably should have been upset about the airplane fiasco and all, I wasn't. Twelve hours ago I had been terrified of college. Since then I had made some new friends and come to the conclusion that things could only go up from here.

—ANDY GOTTESMAN, UNIVERSITY OF MICHIGAN

FIVE TIPS FOR ORIENTATION

For many, orientation week turns out to be the best part of freshman year. No homework. No parents. New environment. New friends. Parties. Parties. More parties.

Besides the fun and games, you will be registering for classes (See Chapter 8, Choosing Classes), taking placement exams, and finding out where you fit into your new home. Here are five tips to help make your orientation experience more fun—and hopefully more fruitful as well.

 Psst . . . Not all schools have the same type of orientation. Some may be three days, others a week. Some might be during the middle of summer, others right before school starts. In addition, the orientation activities will be different at each college.

These hints, however, should help regardless of the type of orientation you attend.

1. MEET AS MANY STUDENTS AS POSSIBLE.

> *I had a friend who decided to stay in her assigned dorm room for most of the orientation. When she came back to school in the fall, she was disappointed because it seemed that everyone else had more friends than she did. She told me that missing the "initial" meeting period during orientation had left her feeling out of place at college.*
>
> *"I'm still being introduced to people that my friends are already acquainted with," she said. "I should have made more of an effort during orientation."*
>
> —FRANCES CARHART, WELLESLEY COLLEGE

Orientation is perhaps the only time when nearly all outside pressures are placed on hold. You won't have any homework or jobs to think about. Take advantage of this and try to make as many new friends as possible. Most of the people you meet will be just as anxious to make new acquaintances as you are.

Don't be afraid to initiate contact with someone you don't know. "Hi, I'm Hugh, from Duluth . . ." is always a good way to start (especially if your name is Hugh!). Don't just hang out with the people you already know from high school. Don't ignore them either, but spread out . . . lest you meet the same fate as the protagonist in the story below.

My friend from home and I stuck together like glue during orientation. We missed home and wanted to stay together.

But hanging out so much at orientation was a bad idea because when we came back in September a lot of other students were always saying, "Oh, you were in my orientation group . . . what's up?" They had built up some sort of foundation already for getting to know new people at school.

Looking back on it, I wish I had done more of that.

—SHARI SOLOMON, UNIVERSITY OF VERMONT

2. EXPLORE THE CAMPUS.

One of the best things to do once you arrive on campus is to gather up some new acquaintances and take your own personal tour of the campus and the surrounding city.

A guided tour will only give you a superficial look at the place you will be spending the next four years. When you go on your own exploration, look for the "grease spots" and unique eateries. These may come in handy later in the fall as alternatives to university food service. If you can, ask some older students which are the best places to visit. They usually will have a pretty good idea of where students hang out.

3. SAMPLE THE NIGHT LIFE AT YOUR COLLEGE.

I was really excited about orientation. Coming from out of state, I arrived early and stayed with my cousin's roommate, Shannon. Although orientation was during summer school, I still wanted to experience the night life. So, Shannon took me to some parties.

Even though I didn't really know anyone, it was a good opportunity for me to test my social (party) skills. I had a good time, but I did learn one thing: Watch out for persistent guys, otherwise known as pick-up artists.

—JESSICA WEINMAN, UC-SANTA BARBARA

Whatever you do, don't lock yourself in your room. Much of college is social, and it would be a shame to ignore that reality during your orientation.

Experiment. Go to a Greek party, even if you don't plan on rushing. Grab a group of newfound friends and sample a local pub in town. In simpler language, have a blast. But, as the student in the previous story mentioned, watch out for those guys who are just waiting to try out their pick-up lines on the newest freshman women in town.

4. ATTEND A FEW WORKSHOPS AND TAKE THE NECESSARY EXAMS.

Your orientation pamphlet undoubtedly will be filled with activities and lectures, which could take up your entire day.

Some of these workshops and/or lectures may prove worthwhile, but it would be a mistake to try to attend every one at the expense of not meeting people. Go to the lectures that seem to be the most interesting and don't worry about the rest.

In addition, don't forget to take the necessary placement exams in math, English, foreign languages, chemistry, and the like. If you plan on taking upper-level courses, some schools require you to pass the placement tests in these areas. Should you study for these exams? Not really. Just give it your best shot, and you'll probably end up where you belong.

5. HAVE FUN...ORIENTATION ONLY COMES ONCE.

It's that simple. Orientation is not a time to worry about classes (except when you are signing up for them) or homework or anything for that matter. It's a time to get a quick glance at your new home and the people that will be living there. Enjoy it. It only comes once.

CHAPTER **7**

Choosing Classes

> The biggest mistake people make when choosing classes is looking at the course titles. They'll take a class like "Abortion and the Supreme Court" or "Suspense in Alfred Hitchcock" just because it sounds interesting. What students should be more concerned with is the professor who is teaching the class—not the class itself.
>
> A bad teacher can make the most interesting subject boring. Similarly, a good teacher can make "Weaving in Ancient Togo" the most fascinating course at college. Ask older students and your advisor who the best teachers are.
>
> Pick exciting professors. You'll end up sleeping through the boring classes anyway.
>
> —GREG GOTTESMAN, STANFORD UNIVERSITY

TEN TIPS ON CHOOSING CLASSES

Most high school students didn't get to choose which courses to take. In college, however, selecting your classes will be invaluable in determining what type of education you receive. Below are 10 ways to help you choose classes—the right way.

1. DON'T OVERBURDEN YOURSELF.

For most students, the first quarter of freshman year marks a time of adjustment. Every freshman is bombarded with a host of new acquaintances, new activities and new responsibilities.

For these reasons, overburdening yourself with a gigantic course load is foolish. You will have plenty of time to take many of the classes listed on the time schedule during later semesters.

At the same time, don't take such a light course load that you won't be challenged. Perhaps the best idea, then, is to take an average course load, which amounts to 15 units or credits at most colleges. In this way, you will not seriously overburden yourself, and you will be able to measure how much time you need to study during an average 15-unit semester.

 Psst . . . Always take enough units so that, if you drop a course (perhaps one that you are failing), you will not go on academic probation. Many schools put a student on academic probation if he or she takes nine units or less. Thus, it is a good idea to always sign up for 14 units or more, so you can drop one five-unit class if necessary.

2. DON'T SIGN UP FOR THREE READING-INTENSIVE COURSES.

Try to vary the type of courses you take, especially freshman year. You don't want to be stuck in the library your first week of school with three readers the size of *War and Peace*.

Instead, try to sign up for one math/science class and two reading-intensive courses or enroll in two math/science classes and one reading-intensive course. Basically, you want to avoid too much reading or too many problem sets.

In terms of specifics, math/science courses would include biology, chemistry, physics and, of course, calculus and geometry.

Reading-intensive courses might include classes in anthropology, English, history, political science, psychology, and various other social sciences.

3. SAMPLE A VARIETY OF SUBJECT AREAS.

> *There are many college courses that you will have never even heard of while in high school. Sociology, psychology, political science, communication, art history . . . the list is endless. You will be cheating yourself if you don't try out some of these new areas of study. You know, it's not uncommon for a pre-med to switch to an art history major after finding out that pre-med is boring and art history is his or her true love.*
>
> —KATIE MACDONALD, UNIVERSITY OF WASHINGTON

If you go to college with your career plans set in stone, you are going to miss out on three-fourths of the "college experience." It's okay to be leaning toward pre-med or political science but don't rule out other subject areas without giving them a chance.

Subjects you enjoyed in high school may not interest you in college. Besides that, you may find academic nirvana in a totally random subject area. Come to college with an open mind; you can always switch back to your original academic plans at a later date.

 Psst . . . If you have your heart set on law school or medical school and think you need to major in a certain area, think again. Law schools, medical schools, and business schools are encouraging students to major in a variety of areas. In other words, you don't need to be an economics major to go to business school. You don't need to be a pre-law major to go to law school. And you don't need to be a biology major to go to medical school; you only need the prerequisites.

4. CHOOSE PROFESSORS, NOT TITLES.

As the first anecdote in this chapter attests, a professor makes a course—not the other way around. Find out who the best professors are and take their classes, especially if they are in your field. Even if they are not in your field, try to get into classes with the best teachers.

 Psst . . . Just because someone is a Nobel laureate does not make him or her a great lecturer or teacher. Sign up for the best teaching professors, not the best researchers.

5. GET YOUR REQUIREMENTS OUT OF THE WAY EARLY.

Don't wait around until senior year to fulfill distribution or language requirements. While freshmen should experiment with a variety of courses, part of your freshman course list should include distribution requirements and/or a language requirement. Come the last quarter of senior year, you are not going to want to be sitting in a Spanish class when you have 15 units of your major to complete.

Besides, university distribution requirements often turn out to be interesting courses, which may lead your education in a totally different direction.

6. TALK WITH OLDER STUDENTS AS WELL AS YOUR ADVISOR.

When choosing classes, there are a multitude of people whom you can consult. You probably will be assigned an advisor, whom you will meet with on a regular basis to discuss course plans. The only problem is that these advisors usually do not have a "pulse" on which are the best courses and who are the best teachers.

Older students in your dorm or Greek house will be able to give you more of the "inside scoop" on many of the classes you are considering. They can tell you who are the interesting professors and who are the duds. Ask as many older stu-

After a speech about how our academic advisors would be assigned based on our own interests, I was told that mine was Barry Nailbuff, a professor in the economics department who was also interested in squash.

I have no interest in either economics or squash.

The next day I met with Barry to discuss the classes I would take first semester and he convinced me to drop my introductory American history course and take Politics 336: Introduction to World Order, taught by Professor Richard Falk.

"Dick and I play squash," he said.

Taking my advisor's advice, I signed up for the class.

It was the worst experience of my life because no freshman mind could hope to comprehend this course.

—JIM GROSSMAN, PRINCETON UNIVERSITY

dents as possible. They will be flattered that someone thinks their opinion means something.

Your advisor and your parents are better suited to deal with your long-term plans, not your immediate course selection.

7. DON'T GET FRUSTRATED IF CLASSES ARE CLOSED.

Despite what other students may say, you usually can get into a course if you are willing to persevere and sit in on the first few class sessions. This, of course, does not include the

Registration isn't always so easy. While I was registering for winter-term classes, I got to the registration room only to find a line about 50 people deep. My registration date was the last one at the university, so I'd listed about twice the number of classes I needed.

I got one—Great Books. I was waitlisted for seven classes. On one list, I was No. 132. That meant I would spend the first couple weeks of the semester sitting in on three sections of the same class and begging the teachers to let me in.

They all did.

Every term since, whether registration has been simple or difficult, I've always ended up getting what I wanted—with a little patience and persistence, I have a funny feeling that's how it works for most people.

—Andy Gottesman, University of Michigan

smaller seminars, which often are reserved for juniors, seniors and graduate students. But large lecture courses tend to let everybody in—eventually. What's one extra body?

8. IF YOU HAVE PROBLEMS, SEEK HUMAN—NOT COMPUTER—ASSISTANCE.

Many larger schools are now letting students register by touch-tone telephone. While this often simplifies the process, don't hesitate to call the registrar's office if you have a problem. This applies to any concerns you are having with registration. Don't wait until classes start to figure out that you are not enrolled in any.

In the spring of 1990, Kent State unveiled its brand-new telephone registration system. The system would supposedly eliminate all the lines, bureaucratic hassles, and confusion of the traditional registration process.

Yeah, right!

By accident, I missed my prearranged time to call in my course selections. But I didn't worry. I had enough credit hours to be a senior, so I would just register during the time left over for seniors.

Wrong! The annoyingly sedated computer voice kept telling me that each class would put me over the number of allowable credit hours. What?

When I finally talked to someone who knew what they were doing, I found out the problem was that the computer had listed my "hours allowable" at zero. I guess they really didn't want me to come back to school.

—Matt Kelly, Kent State University

9. DON'T WORRY ABOUT A MAJOR JUST YET.

Nobody will be asking you to declare a major as soon as you get to college. As a matter of fact, most advisors will discourage it.

There are many questions that you need to answer before choosing a major. What kind of job are you planning on? Do you wish to attend graduate school?

But these questions can all be answered after freshman year, after you have decided what you like and after you have figured out the subjects in which you excel.

Remember once again that your major does not necessarily dictate your future career.

10. STAY CALM AND SIGN UP FOR SOME FUN COURSES.

Freshman year is a time to experiment; it's also a time to have a little fun. If you see a course that sounds interesting, try it out. You can always drop it if you don't like the first class session.

Most importantly, relax. Study hard but remember . . . you have three more years to worry about a major.

CHAPTER **8**

Time Management and Study Tactics

> *How did the guy do it? He never studied. He was always asking everyone to shoot hoops, to throw the football, to crash that fraternity party, to go and hear Senator Joe Biden . . . but he got straight A's. I couldn't figure it out.*
>
> *Then it happened. I was up late doing research in the library. It was approaching midnight, but I wanted to read a few more pages on the joys of microbiology. So, I looked for the most secluded place in the library in which to stash myself and read to my heart's content. Lo and behold, there he was—Mr. Joe Cool—hitting the books like book burners were going to storm in tomorrow.*
>
> *I yelled over to him, "Caught you!" He laughed, but I knew he was a bit disappointed. That day I realized, to be successful socially and academically in college, everyone needs to learn to manage their time appropriately. Of course, not everyone has to do it the same way.*
>
> —Brandon Hsu, Stanford University

Finding Time for Everything

As you will soon find out, college offers much more than studying. In fact, finding time for everything without

55

neglecting the books may be the most challenging test a college student faces.

CLASSWORK: WHAT TO EXPECT

The days when teachers looked over your shoulder and nagged you about homework and tests are past. In many classes, especially at larger schools, you are just a face in a crowd of 500—a "number," as the expression goes. Teachers assume you are sufficiently responsible to keep up with your work without individual attention.

The structure of most college courses reflects this philosophy. Instead of daily graded assignments and monthly tests, most college professors evaluate students solely on the basis of a midterm and a final exam or a midterm exam and a term project. Homework, more often than not, is optional while reading assignments are longer and less structured. For example, instead of saying, "Read these 10 pages for tomorrow," the professor will remark, "Read this book before the next mid-term."

Just as often, the professor will not say anything about assignments but rely on the syllabus given to each student the first day of class. This item—the syllabus—is invaluable; keep it in a safe place.

With classwork structured in this way, falling behind tends to haunt anyone with the slightest lazy streak. The laid-back student may find himself approaching the midterm or even the final without having read or written anything. For those who crammed in high school (and succeeded), try cramming for a final on Dostoyevsky's *The Brothers Karamozov*, Nietzsche's *Beyond Good and Evil*, Camus' *The Stranger*, Sartre's *No Exit*, and Kafka's *The Trial*—and that's just for starters. Needless to say, time management plays a large role in any successful college career.

HOMEWORK: HOW TO STAY ON TOP

Self-discipline and organization are the keys to avoiding the pitfalls of procrastination. Below are a few clues to help in this war against putting things off.

1. PLOT YOUR TIME WITH A CALENDAR.

During the first week of classes, sit with a calendar and the syllabus from each class. Mark each test, paper, and assignment date, particularly noting those that fall within a day or two of each other. Such occasions are not uncommon and require extra planning. Arco's *College Time Tracker* is indispensable when it comes to tackling these full weeks.

Dr. Lauren Cohen, who has taught study strategies for 20 years at the college level, recommends plotting your course of action on a calendar. "Set daily and weekly goals on a calendar. If something comes up unexpectedly like a date, borrow time from another day, even if it means getting up an hour earlier. Marking specific deadlines on a chart and making sure to meet them enhances one's chance for success."

Expect to spend at least two nights studying for any significant exam. Papers may require more time if research is needed. Also, allow extra time to type and print your paper, especially if computer resources are limited. Finally, don't get behind in your other classes while concentrating on one. Work ahead in the others before favoring a particular class.

 Psst . . . Many students play catch-up all year. You know the game—teacher explains one section, you read it two weeks later. Dumb! By reading the assignments before class, the lecture material is clearer and easier to absorb. You are going to have to read the stuff anyway.

2. ATTEND CLASS TO BOOST THE OLE G.P.A.

Much in the same regard as homework, college professors assume students are disciplined enough to attend class on a regular basis. While in smaller classes professors may be concerned with frequent student absence, few professors take role and even fewer figure attendance into the course grade. But don't let this lax attitude give you an excuse to sleep through your morning classes or bask in the sun on warm afternoons. Class attendance is critical to college success.

Whatever you do, don't let those few Einsteins who can ace a test by never attending class and by sleeping on the text book the night before trick you into using their study methods. My roommate tried to convince me that studying by osmosis was a proven method. Trust me, it isn't. In other words, just because someone can do well on a test without going to class or even looking at the book doesn't mean you can do the same.

—KEITH VERNON, UNIVERSITY OF PUGET SOUND

Copying notes from a more disciplined friend will not suffice. Notes should be used as an outline, reminding you of key concepts and theories covered in class. Borrowed notes will give you facts and figures but won't paint the complete picture of how the facts and figures interrelate. So, set the alarm, save the sun for the weekend, and go to class with pen and paper in hand.

If you have time, read your lecture notes at the end of each day or at least the end of the week. Students who do this find they do not have to study as much come finals week because the material already has been planted firmly in their minds.

Psst . . . According to the Ebbinghaus Retention Curve, you lose more than 50 percent of processed information within one hour of leaving the classroom. You surrender 60 to 70 percent within 24 hours. After 30 days, 70 percent is gone.

Reviewing, rewriting, and discussing classwork is the only way to effectively counteract this phenomenon. The more you engage with the material, the more you retain.

3. LEARN HOW TO STUDY EFFECTIVELY.

Face the facts! Colleges and universities are institutions of higher learning for those who want to learn. Professors expect you to study; parents expect you to study; you should expect yourself to study. Indeed, studying is a foregone conclusion. Why not make the most of it?

Okay, you're ready to hit the books for that big exam. What do you do?

First, find a suitable study environment. Some like soft music in the background. Some need people around. For most, however, a comfortable chair in a quiet room works best. Regardless, make sure you are in a place free of the temptation to socialize. Dorm rooms, particularly when shared with a roommate, seldom meet this requirement. The basement of the library or an abandoned classroom are much more accommodating.

By the way, don't fall asleep. Sleep is undoubtedly your biggest enemy. And don't study in bed; it's the kiss of death. Twenty minutes of reading in bed and, bye-bye, you've had it!

One way to avoid sleeping when you want to be studying is to use breaks as incentives. Say to yourself, "I'll go talk to some friends after I finish this chapter," or, "After I finish my chemistry, I can go out for some frozen yogurt." Don't break too often or you will frustrate your concentration and cause further distraction.

Dr. Cohen recommends working for 50 minutes and breaking for 10.

If you still have trouble getting things done or find yourself asking, "What have I been doing these last two hours?" when you were supposedly studying, make a daily schedule. Figure out what you have to do in each class, calculate how long each task will take and set up a timetable, allotting time for breaks as well.

 Psst . . . Remember to highlight important points in the chapters you read. It makes studying before a test so much easier.

4. PROCRASTINATION: AVOID THE INEVITABLE.

At one time or another, every college student will get behind in his or her work—no matter how disciplined or diligent the person. A curious quirk of college life is that, come finals week, bragging rights belong to the student with the most work and the least time to complete it. Although the struggle to stay afloat in the sea of academia challenges every student, it should not be used as an excuse to drown.

> *I had a friend who was concentrating in pre-med. He put off studying for his chem midterm until 10 P.M. the night before, spending his time instead at the movies and the campus hang-out. After bombing the exam, he told us he did not have enough time to study. Basically, he gave himself an excuse to fail.*
>
> —THOM MCDADE, POMONA COLLEGE

Any student can put off his or her work until it reaches unconquerable proportions. Any student can fail. The successful student sees work not as a chore, but as a means of testing his or her potential.

IF ALL ELSE FAILS . . . PULL AN ALL-NIGHTER!

> *I never pulled an all-nighter in high school. I think the latest I ever stayed up was about 3 A.M. All that changed when I went to the University of Texas.*
>
> *Austin is a 24-hour party town. In between the "Hook 'em Horns" football games and the jazz clubs on Sixth Street, I hardly had time to sleep, let alone work on papers all week.*
>
> *So when it came time to write a big paper, I basically just planned on staying up all night. In my first semester at UT, I probably pulled . . . oh . . . about seven or eight all-nighters. Some people might say I was going overboard, but at UT that's just a way of life.*
>
> —CATHERINE CHEN, UNIVERSITY OF TEXAS AT AUSTIN

Thus far, this chapter has preached the values of good time management. Indeed, nothing is more essential for continued college success. But regardless of how diligent you are, there are going to be instances when time is simply not on your side.

With so many extracurricular activities going on at college, along with classes, most students find themselves overwhelmed at certain points during the year. Fear not! For times like these, college students around the globe have invented a new concept in last-minute studying: the all-nighter.

For the most part, an all-nighter consists of staying up all night (or as late as need be) to complete a paper, finish a project or study for a test. But willpower alone will not pull you through the wee hours. From Tulane University in New Orleans to Oxford University in England, students have turned the all-nighter into an art form. Here are five tips to help make you an artist.

FIVE TIPS FOR PULLING THE ALL-NIGHTER

1. GRAB SOME FOOD AND CAFFEINE, BUT KEEP IT TO A MINIMUM.

> *Food and stimulants are helpful to keep you going—but only in moderation. I remember once I was pulling an all-nighter to finish a research paper. Meanwhile, I had my Mr. Coffee Jr. brewing up several bucket loads of full-strength DuMond Chickory coffee. I also had a pack of fudge-covered Oreos, which I had bought in preparation for the long night.*
>
> *Three pots of coffee and a package of cookies later, I was sick to my stomach, bouncing off the walls, and staring at a vague outline. After wasting another hour or two in transit to and from the bathroom, I calmed myself down and got to work. A paper I could have finished by the early hours of the morning turned into a long and desperate project.*
>
> —STEVE BLUMENTHAL, TULANE UNIVERSITY

Don't underestimate the value of coffee, a sandwich, a chocolate-chip cookie or a pack of M&Ms at 4 A.M. when the ideas aren't flowing. You may even want to plan ahead and purchase a few selected favorites from the college store before commencing with the all-nighter.

But whatever you do, don't drink so much caffeine or gobble down so much sugar that you're ready for outer space. Caffeine, while helping you to stay awake, also can give you the jitters. Keep it to a minimum.

2. DON'T GO NEAR YOUR BED.

> *It was 12:30 A.M. I was sleepy. But I couldn't hit the hay for another five or six hours because I had this organic chemistry midterm in the morning and a lot more studying to do.*
>
> *I decided to study on my bed because my desk was getting uncomfortable. Big mistake. No, HUGE mistake. The next thing I know, I look over at the clock: 9:50 A.M.! All the lights are still on, the radio is still playing, and I've got 10 minutes before a chemistry midterm, which I haven't studied for. When it came time for the final later that term, I studied at my desk—the whole time!*
>
> —KIMARA LEIBOWITZ, BROWN UNIVERSITY

Sleep is your greatest nightmare when trying to pull an all-nighter. How to avoid Freddie Kreuger?

Stay away from your bed, at all costs. If possible, stay away from your room. Study in your dorm's kitchen or in the library. And, if you can help it, avoid taking naps. Many a student has lain down to grab a few Z's only to wake up a few minutes before test time!

3. MAKE AN OUTLINE EARLY ON.

At 3:30 A.M., many students' minds start wandering to the sandy, spring break beaches of Mexico. So, particularly if you're going to spend the whole night writing a paper, it's a good idea to have a rough outline of the essay before you start. A general outline will give your essay some needed order. This is essential since "logical progression" is one of the first things to go when the clock strikes twelve.

Psst . . . If you're studying for a test in the wee hours of the morning, take notes. Writing down the material on paper will help your short-term memory recall facts and figures come test time later in the day.

4. GIVE YOURSELF INCENTIVES TO CONTINUE.

> *My friends and I did some weird things to help us stay awake the night before a big paper was due. I remember once my roommate and I decided to put on our formal dresses— we're talking cinched waist, straight-skirt, fitted bodice, totally uncomfortable—and promised ourselves that we wouldn't take them off until we had finished. Needless to say, those were two papers we finished in a hurry.*
>
> —HEATHER WOLFE, AMHERST COLLEGE

Incentives work extremely well when you've still got six pages to write and the motivation to write only two. That doesn't mean you have to put on formal attire. Other incentives, like telling yourself that a cup of coffee awaits after you finish another page, are always helpful.

5. DON'T STRESS OUT.

All-nighters are a part of college life. Enjoy them. Revel in the fact that, after four years, you probably will never pull an all-nighter again—at least not for studying purposes. The worst thing you can do is stress out. Grab some food and drink and make a night out of it. In a nutshell, see the all-nighter as an adventure, not a job.

> *My American friend, Red, defined the term "stressing out." Before every tutorial, he would carry on: "Ohmigod, what am I going to do? I can't handle this. I'm going to flunk out. Help!" Finally, someone would calm him down, but he could have accomplished a lot more if he just relaxed a little. I guess that's the American spirit for you, or at least Red's.*
>
> —SCOTT PARKER, OXFORD UNIVERSITY

SIX QUICK TEST-TAKING TIPS

College Survival has given you a few tips on how to prepare for tests. Here are a few essential suggestions on what to do while taking the actual exam.

1. LIVE FOR PARTIAL CREDIT.

Always show your work. If worst comes to worse, write *something* down, anything, even if it's your girlfriend's phone number as opposed to the correct answer. Partial credit has salvaged more than a few test scores, especially in science courses where the median score is often 40 percent or lower.

2. USE KEY WORDS AND CATCH PHRASES.

With 400 exam books to grade, a professor or teaching assistant is usually not worrying about the intricacies of your test. In fact, the grader may just have a checklist with key words and catch phrases on it. If your essay has a lot of these key words you may earn an "A" or "B," if not, you may receive a "C" or "D." Ugh!

3. WRITE CLEARLY.

No, this doesn't mean use good handwriting (although some professors demand it). It means write with clarity and purpose. The object is simple but contradictory: Get down as much as possible in the most logical fashion.

4. ALWAYS AGREE.

Unless you *really* know your stuff, don't disagree with the teacher. Regurgitation, however boring, is your best bet come report card time.

5. ANSWER EVERY QUESTION, IF POSSIBLE.

Don't spend two hours answering the first question when you have five more of equal weight staring you in the face. Bide your time and make sure to answer most completely those questions that are worth the most points.

6. DON'T STRESS OUT.

Getting uptight because you can't answer the first question is futile. Move on. If the rest of the test looks like Chinese when it's supposed to be Spanish, do the best you can. Try rewording the questions so they make more sense to you. Chances are, other students are having the same problems you are.

Excessive worrying only makes you less productive. If all else fails, refer to Tip No. 1 and pray.

CHAPTER 9

Setting Goals For Success

> *I did a lot of goofing-off in high school. While some of my friends were studying, I'd be out shooting hoops or playing cards or the like. But all this goofing-off put me in the doghouse when it came time to choose colleges.*
>
> *Most of my friends went to the University of Washington, but because of my grades, I didn't have that option. I chose the University of Portland.*
>
> *From the start, I decided that I wanted to be with my friends and transfer to Washington. So, I called up the U.W. admissions office and asked what type of grades I needed to transfer. They told me I needed a 3.3. So, for the first semester at Portland, my bookbag was my girlfriend. The library was my Friday night party palace.*
>
> *When grades for first semester came out, I did a double-take: 3.9! What's this? Get Harvard on the line.*
>
> *It just goes to show what having a goal and following through can do. A 2.5 in high school to a 3.9 in college—even I wouldn't have put money on that one.*
>
> —CHRIS SCALZO, UNIVERSITY OF PORTLAND

THE FIVE BASIC STEPS OF GOAL SETTING

Successful college students, regardless of the institution they attend, use these five steps to set goals:

1. Make a scale of priorities
2. Set measurable and realistic long-term goals
3. Set short-term goals
4. Make social, personal and academic goals
5. Strive to meet those goals.

Goal setting does not necessarily mean sitting down with pen and paper and making a list of priorities, although often that can be extremely helpful. At the very least, however, goal setting should become a regular mental exercise.

> *I have never actually written down a set of goals, but I still go through the process of "goal setting" everyday. I'm always asking myself, "How am I going to get an 'A' on this next test? What is the best way to prepare? Am I going to have to skip playing tennis tomorrow to make time for studying?"*
>
> *Goal setting, as far as I can see it, is simply a state of mind, a way of thinking about things. A goal setter makes sure he accomplishes what he needs to accomplish. He takes the necessary steps in that direction.*
>
> *College is full of distractions. In fraternities, sororities and dorms, there are always TVs blaring, people to talk to, and parties of some sort every night. It's very easy for someone who hasn't set priorities to get sidetracked.*
>
> —GREG GOTTESMAN, STANFORD UNIVERSITY

 Psst . . . Dr. Lauren Cohen, a college professor of 20 years, recommends physically writing down long-term and short-term goals. She has done this with many students and insists that it enhances one's chance for success.

1. MAKE A SCALE OF YOUR PRIORITIES.

By now, after 17-plus years, you have established a certain lifestyle. Perhaps you are a student, an athlete, a musician, a partier, or a combination of all of these. Without even knowing it, you have set priorities and lived by them.

College is the time to look at who you are and contrast what you see with who you want to become. This does not mean you shouldn't be yourself but, rather, that you should make room for growth and improvement.

For example, if you were a partier in high school but want to become more of a student, now is the time to change. If you were not an athlete but want to learn how to play tennis, now is the time to sign up. If you always wanted to hold a school office but never had the chance, now is the time to get involved on campus or in the community.

By making a scale of what is important, you will be ready to set some definite goals.

2. SET MEASURABLE AND REALISTIC LONG-TERM GOALS.

Just saying you want to "do well" in school is not enough. Everyone wants to do well. Besides, "doing well" is not a measurable goal; what exactly is "doing well"? Is it an "A" or a "B"?

On a similar note, setting your sights on a 4.0 G.P.A. when you never received above a 2.0 in high school is unrealistic, albeit admirable.

In the simplest of terms, set measurable and reasonable long-term goals. Say to yourself, "I am going to get at least a 'B' in biology," or "I am going to get at least a 3.3 G.P.A." Both of these statements are reasonable and measurable.

3. SET SHORT-TERM GOALS.

Without short-term goals, long-term ones are impossible to achieve.

> *I had a friend who told me at the beginning of the year he would get an 'A' in chemistry. But he ended up just being a talker. For him, just having the goal was good enough.*
>
> —THOM MCDADE, POMONA COLLEGE

To achieve the long-term goal of an "A" in chemistry, this student needed short-term goals. They might have included:

1. Completing all lab assignments
2. Attending all classes
3. Finding a study partner
4. Completing course readings on time
5. Studying hard for the mid-term and final

Even though you may have trouble meeting all these short-term goals, following through on most of them will help you to achieve your long-term aspirations.

4. SET SOCIAL, PERSONAL AND ACADEMIC GOALS.

Academics is only one facet of your college education. You should set social and personal goals as well as academic ones.

For most students, socializing figures high on the priority list . . . only four years left before bellyflopping into the real world, right?

Some of these social ambitions may include dating, getting along with your roommate, becoming more culturally aware, and learning to feel more comfortable in social situations.

As with academic goals, you should subdivide long-term social aspirations into short-term ones. Finding a steady date might be broken down into shorter steps such as going out with several different people or going to at least one party a week.

Personal goals, on the other hand, may consist of balancing your checkbook each month, exercising regularly, or eating a balanced diet.

5. CONTINUALLY STRIVE TO MEET YOUR GOALS.

My friend Gary really wants to study medicine. He is a brilliant guy, and he will make a fantastic surgeon, I'm sure. However, Gary made the mistake of having a bit too much fun his first few years at Rice and pretty much blew off a lot of his school work. He ended up with a 3.0 G.P.A. at the end of his fifth semester, which is at the lower end of the spectrum for the competitive medical schools.

Gary realized he would have to do something to redeem himself, so he spent the entire second semester of his junior year studying for the MCAT to be held that April. No more partying for Gary; he attended only two social events that semester and spent every other minute reviewing biology, chemistry and physics. Needless to say, Gary breezed through the test.

Most of Gary's friends think he is insane for giving up four months of his life studying for a test. But Gary thinks he got a pretty good deal: studying like a madman for one term in exchange for a future.

—ROSALIND MARTZ, RICE UNIVERSITY

Think of how few people ever achieve their dream of becoming a Hollywood star, an olympic champion, or the C.E.O. of a large corporation. Obviously, no one is giving away free tickets to success. However, by prioritizing, by setting realistic long-term goals and by achieving long-term goals through short-term ones, you will be surprised at how much you can accomplish.

As Alfred, Lord Tennyson once said, " 'Tis better to have loved and lost / than never to have loved at all." Well, you know what he meant: Go for it!

CHAPTER **10**
Getting Involved

> When I arrived at La Salle, I was a little afraid to devote too much time to extracurriculars. I wasn't sure how much time I would have after classes and homework and parties. What I didn't realize was how much more free time I would have in college. Granted, I had more homework than in high school, but with fewer classes in college I also had more time to get it done.
>
> Joining the newspaper was one of the best decisions I made. I met some of my best friends on the staff—two of my roommates and a boyfriend! It also gave me something else to do besides school work. My friends who just concentrated on academics really missed out.
>
> —CHRISTINA ROACHE, LA SALLE UNIVERSITY

WILL I HAVE TIME TO GET INVOLVED?

Believe it or not, you're going to have a bunch of free time in college. In high school, the majority of your day was spent in the classroom. Not so in college. Most freshmen average only three hours a day in lecture; the rest of your day is yours.

Although college courses require more study time, it would be a mistake to be on a first-name basis with the local librarian. Activities outside of your course work will be just as important to your "college experience."

What Can I Get Involved In?

Most colleges offer every type of activity you have ever imagined and even some you haven't. Experiment! Try a variety of activities, some you may have done in high school and others that just sound interesting. Dan Hutter from the University of Miami said, "Don't be afraid to go a little bit wild. If newspaper and student government don't excite you, there's a lot else out there. Skydiving . . . now that's something Mom and Dad can tell their friends about."

If you're afraid of heights, here is a list of some of the more traditional extracurriculars:

- SPORTS: You don't need to be a varsity athlete to exercise (See *Chapter 16* for details).

- BAND: If you played an instrument in high school and enjoyed it, join the band or another musical group. It's a great way to see football games for free.

- POLITICS: If you're a budding politician, your school's student government will have numerous elected and committee positions. Working for a cause or on a local politician's campaign are two other options.

- JOURNALISM: If you enjoy writing, there are a lot of different student publications on campus. Some even pay you to write. Great way to make some extra money!

- ARTS: Whether you are a performer or just a connoisseur, college will offer you a host of cultural opportunities in music, dance and theater. Just because you didn't act or dance in high school doesn't mean you shouldn't try now. Many theaters offer college students the opportunity to usher and see top-rate cultural events for free.

WHY GET INVOLVED?

> *Getting involved with College Republicans was the best decision I made in college. I came to Boston University unsure of my abilities. College Republicans gave me confidence in myself. After holding several leadership positions in the group, I was elected to the National Office of the College Republicans my senior year. The leadership skills I learned in that group will help me for the rest of my life.*
>
> —WILLIAM SPADEA, BOSTON UNIVERSITY

1. MAKE FRIENDS.

Usually your best friends in college will be those people who have similar interests. For that reason, extracurriculars are a great place to make lasting friendships and find future roommates.

2. RELIEVE STRESS.

Extracurriculars offer a legitimate break from the grind of schoolwork. Shooting hoops or playing in the band will let you return to Plato in a better frame of mind.

3. BUILD A RESUME.

Extracurriculars may give you some ideas about future career paths. In addition, getting involved in group activities will teach you cooperation, organization and leadership skills. At the very least, extracurriculars are very important for an effective resume. Would you hire someone with a 4.0 average and the personality of a No. 2 pencil?

4. HAVE FUN.

Let's face it, unless you're an ancient philosopher, reading books can get kind of boring. Enough said.

WILL IT HARM MY GRADES?

Contrary to what you might think, getting involved won't necessarily hurt your grades. In fact, studies have shown the opposite: people who are more involved tend to get better grades. They organize their time better and study more efficiently. As Walt Eife of Western Maryland College said, "The more things I have to do during a day, the more I get done. If I don't have anything, I just watch TV and save all my work till the last minute."

WHAT ABOUT COMMUNITY SERVICE?

If you're only going to participate in one extracurricular activity, consider community service. The rewards are incredible.

Most campuses have a community service center where you can get information about different projects. Some of these activities might include working on the Special Olympics, tutoring economically disadvantaged students or building shelters for the homeless.

In the past, college students have been responsible for much positive change in our society. More than any group, they have the free time, energy and optimism to truly make a difference.

I remember how scared I was the first time I visited the juvenile jail. I figured I'd meet a lot of tough kids who wouldn't be interested in doing any of the activities we had planned for them.

For the first few hours, my worst fears were confirmed. They laughed at the idea of freeze tag, rolled their eyes at making montages and refused to do pantomimes. I was getting discouraged, to put it mildly.

Then I sat down with one of the girls and just started talking. After a while she began to open up and tell me about her past. She never knew her father, and her mom was in prison for prostitution. She herself was in jail for drug pushing, the only work she could find at age 12. When I first sat down, I thought I could teach her something about life. Little did I know I'd be the person to learn.

After that initial bonding, the girls were more excited about our games. The next few hours passed quickly and soon it was time to go. The girl I had spoken with came over and gave me the biggest hug. She told me that she had never had so much fun in her life and made me promise I'd come back. I have never felt quite like that again.

—TARA McCANN, STANFORD UNIVERSITY

At Stanford, it's very easy to get caught up in the palm trees, the academics, the people. I know a lot of students who spend four years here without ever leaving the campus. Kind of sad!

For that reason, I have made a concerted effort to try to get out in the community and help out. I teach tennis and physical education to high school and elementary school students in East Palo Alto. It's the most rewarding thing I've done for several reasons. It keeps me in touch with the real world. It makes me feel good about myself. It also gives me the chance to make an impact on real people. You'd be surprised how much impact you can have on the life of a fifth grader.

—GREG GOTTESMAN, STANFORD UNIVERSITY

CHAPTER 11

Computers at College

> *Possessing a mortal fear of my dormitory's computer cluster, I insisted on using my friend's Apple IIc whenever I needed a paper typed.*
>
> *Borrowing my friend's computer was not intrinsically evil. The only problem is . . . I'm a terrible procrastinator. I cannot even count the number of all-nighters I pulled in front of that green-glowing screen, while my pal slept uncomfortably through the god-awful sounds of clicking computer keys.*
>
> *It got so bad that by the end of the year my friend began shouting sarcastic remarks at me in his sleep, such as: "James, could you type a little louder please!" That was about the same time I realized I had worn out my welcome and needed a computer of my own.*
>
> —JAMES REYNOLDS, STANFORD UNIVERSITY

THE CONVENIENCE OF COMPUTING

Computers, with on-screen editing, electronic spell-checking, and built-in thesauruses have made typewriters as obsolete as Sanskrit. The choice is no longer between using a computer and not using one; it's whether you own one or use someone else's.

COMPUTER LINGO

Hardware: Computer, monitor, disk drives, printer, mouse, modem, and cables.

Software: Software, often called programs or applications, are the instructions that a computer needs to perform a task like word processing or playing a game.

Mouse: A small box-shaped device you slide over a desktop or a "mouse pad" to move a pointer on a computer's screen.

Kilobyte (K or kb), Megabyte (meg or mb), Gigabyte (G or gb): These terms refer to quantities of information. A byte is about one character, a kilobyte about 1,000, a megabyte about one million, and a gigabyte about one trillion.

Floppy disk: Removable magnetic disk enclosed in a square protective cover of 5 $1/4$ inches (soft cover) or 3 $1/2$ inches (hard plastic cover). These disks come in regular and high density. The 3 $1/2$ inch high-density disks (1.44 mb) are now the industry standard.

Hard disk: Nonremovable magnetic disk contained within a computer used to store multiple programs and large amounts of data and text. Hard disks come in different sizes (megabytes or gigabytes), according to the amount of information they store.

Random Access Memory (RAM): *Temporary* storage area inside a computer. You need more RAM to run complex programs like Microsoft Windows.

Modem: A device for transporting electronic information via telephone.

Baud: The rate at which a modem can send or accept information.

Compact Disk-Read Only Memory (CD-ROM): A small

plastic disk like a music CD that comes with programs, games, and/or music. CD-ROMs have much more memory than a floppy disk, but you cannot save information to a CD-ROM.

BACK TO THE BASICS!

Most personal computers used in college today fall into two categories: IBM-compatibles running Windows programs and Apple Macintoshes (Macs). Stick with one of these two systems. Both are relatively easy to use, and students can find good deals on IBM-compatibles or low-cost Macs. Although Mac software cannot be run on IBM-compatibles and vice versa, some data and text files can be converted back and forth with conversion programs—but not always easily.

With a modem, both IBM-compatibles and Macs can access college library databases, the Internet, and on-line services, such as America Online, CompuServe, and The Microsoft Network.

> *My friend had an Apple IIc from home. Tragically, his only disk drive malfunctioned the night before his first term paper was due. His disks were unreadable by the school's IBMs and Macs. Worse yet, he couldn't find another Apple IIc until the paper's deadline had passed. He was penalized a grade for circumstances seemingly beyond his control.*
>
> —DAN GOTTESMAN, UNIVERSITY OF WASHINGTON

EIGHT BASIC QUESTIONS TO CONSIDER WITH COMPUTERS

1. DO I ALREADY OWN AN ADEQUATE COMPUTER SYSTEM?

If your main goal is to write college papers, almost any IBM-compatible running Windows programs or Mac is adequate.

If you do not own an adequate computer, you can purchase a Mac or IBM-compatible system with pre-installed CD-ROM, modem, color monitor, and ink-jet printer for less than $2,000. Your computer should include a minimum of eight megs of RAM and a 540 or greater megabyte hard drive.

Another important feature for college computers is a modem. A modem allows you to hookup via telephone with most college libraries, send electronic mail (e-mail), and surf the Internet. You should consider at least a 14,400 baud modem (or, for a little more money, a 28,800 baud modem). Most new systems come with internally mounted modems.

2. WHAT ABOUT PRINTERS?

You have three options for printers: dot-matrix, ink-jet, and laser. All are available for both IBM-compatibles and Macs.

Dot-matrix is an older technology and even the newer 24-pin dot-matrix printers cannot compare in quality to ink-jet or laser printers. Don't buy one!

Ink-jet printers are probably the most popular printer type on campuses today. The ink-jets now are priced so competitively that you simply cannot justify buying a dot-matrix printer. Color ink-jet technology is improving steadily, but you don't need color. Professors are not going to bump up your grade for a rainbow on your cover sheet.

Laser printers are the most costly of the three types, and their quality is the best. Some students choose to buy a laser printer over an ink-jet printer and spend less on their computer. The rationale: the professor (or an employer for a resume) only sees your final output, which is determined by your printer (and brain), not the computer. If you are on a budget, however, an ink-jet is more than adequate.

 Psst . . . Don't fret if your printer is not a laser, and you need to print out resumes or a term paper. Most schools have student-use laser printers, which you can use for a small fee.

3. DOES THE SCHOOL PROVIDE SUFFICIENT COMPUTER FACILITIES?

Many colleges offer easily accessible computer facilities in the dormitories or libraries. For the student on a tight budget, it pays to investigate. See if your school has adequate facilities. If the computer facilities are particularly good, you may not need your own computer.

Dorm-based computer centers may be ideal for the nonowner. Call the housing office once you have received your assignment and ask about computer availability. Even if you buy one, it's nice to have a backup as close as the basement.

Make sure that there are enough facilities to accommodate a good number of students. Come term paper time, you don't want to find yourself at the old-fashioned typewriter because all the terminals are booked.

4. WHAT TYPE OF COMPUTER DOES MOST OF THE CAMPUS USE?

Although few schools will dictate which type of computer students should use, a certain type usually emerges as the "most popular." Dartmouth and Stanford, for example, are Mac schools. Amherst is an IBM-compatible school.

There are numerous benefits to owning the campus' computer of choice. In case of a computer breakdown, there will be more compatible systems that are easily accessible.

5. DOES MY MAJOR REQUIRE A SPECIAL COMPUTER?

Engineering and computer science students may have special computer needs, whereas English and history majors may need to use only simple word processing programs. Check the standards of your department before buying. A $6,000 Mac or IBM-compatible system may be overkill if all you have to do is crank out three papers a quarter.

6. ARE USED COMPUTERS A REASONABLE ALTERNATIVE?

Used systems of *recognized* brand names (e.g., IBM, Compaq, AST, Macintosh) may be good buys, but beware! Technology changes so quickly and the computer market is so competitive that newer and faster systems with warranties and even free servicing are not much more expensive than used ones.

Don't ask a used-computer seller what the system originally cost. That doesn't matter — you need to find out how much the system is worth today! A two-year old system may work fine and have cost $3,000, but might be a bad buy compared to a *new* computer that's twice as fast and half as expensive. Price out new computers before you buy an old one.

For a nominal fee, used computers can be checked out for internal damage by a local computer repair facility. Obscure brands may not be repairable and are not worth the risk.

7. SHOULD I BUY A PORTABLE COMPUTER?

Portable (or laptop) computers have a lot of advantages—and disadvantages. New ones are just as powerful as the computers that sit on your desk, yet they are small enough to fit into your backpack. Portability is a huge plus. You can bring a laptop computer with you to the library to write a paper or into the classroom to take notes.

The major disadvantage of a laptop computer is price. Expect to pay about 50% more for portability. In addition, the screen and keyboard on portable computers are smaller and less friendly than on larger desktop computers. Another major problem is theft. If you can transport your computer comfortably in your backpack, so can someone else. If you buy a portable computer, be careful not to leave your computer alone in public.

8. WHERE SHOULD I BUY A NEW COMPUTER?

Many college bookstores and technology centers offer special student discounts on computers and printers. Check out these prices before buying from other computer stores or looking in the newspaper. One of the advantages of buying on campus is that computer repair is usually easily accessible.

Mail-order purchases may save you a few bucks and sales tax, but be sure to investigate the company before buying over the phone. The best mail-order firms, such as Gateway, Dell, and ZEOS, usually offer good prices and phone service support.

USE AND ABUSE OF COMPUTERS

See James type his term paper on a computer. See James not save his work to the disk. See a power outage in the dorm. See James say bye-bye to his entire paper. See James cry.

James Reynolds, a Stanford junior who typed one extra term paper into the computer, has compiled a list of tips to make sure your computer days are happier than his.

1. BE SURE TO SAVE YOUR WORK EVERY 10 MINUTES.

The computer doesn't permanently record your work until you tell it to. Until then, your paper is at the mercy of the local power company. Don't play the "it won't happen to me" game—because it will.

2. KEEP YOUR COMPUTER IN A COOL PLACE AND AWAY FROM FOOD.

Computers located too close to a vent or radiator may decide to take the day off due to heat exhaustion. Soda pop, milk, and beer also have contributed to many a system's downfall. Magnets are a bad idea, too. Keep them far away from your computer and floppy disks.

3. WHEN BORROWING, ALLOW YOURSELF PLENTY OF TIME.

Woe to the student who needs to borrow a friend's computer only to be told that the friend has 700 resumes to print out before morning.

Establish a borrowing policy early in the year. The owner has the final word.

4. FAMILIARIZE YOURSELF WITH THE SOFTWARE AND HARDWARE.

Don't wait until your first paper to discover you haven't a clue how to run a word processor. Computers can save loads of time if you know how to use them. Some programs have training systems built in. Classes on various aspects of computer use are available at most schools as well.

5. GET TO KNOW A COMPUTER GURU.

You know who they are. Those students who never lose papers, whose megacomputers seem to take up an entire room. There is no magic involved—these folks really know what they're doing, and they're usually glad to help you out of a computer bind.

6. DON'T LET THE COMPUTER BECOME AN ENEMY.

Franklin Delano Roosevelt said it best: "The only thing you have to fear is fear itself." If Frank hadn't had political ambitions, he probably could have been a computer programmer.

Don't let that little glowing screen become an adversary. If you plan correctly, the computer can become your most useful tool at college—next to your brain.

CHAPTER **12**
The Minority Experience

> *I was a little bit apprehensive about my first Indian Students Association meeting. As a freshman, I didn't know any of the other students, and I didn't know what to expect. But once the meeting started, I realized it really wasn't bad. Since my first meeting, I've developed some of my closest friendships with other members that are based on our common experiences as South Asians in America.*
>
> *If you're a minority student, I definitely would recommend going to some of the functions. It makes the university a little less intimidating.*
>
> —ANITHA VENUGOPAL, CORNELL UNIVERSITY

NO "SINGLE" MINORITY EXPERIENCE

Writing a chapter about the minority experience is difficult because there is no "single" minority experience in college (or anywhere else for that matter). The goal of this chapter, then, is not to define the minority experience, but to provide a list of issues for minority students to think about and perhaps to offer a few words of wisdom from those who have been there before. In this chapter, the term "minority" is used broadly to encompass women, students of color, students of different religions, and students who are gay, lesbian, or bisexual.

MINORITY GROUP ACTIVITIES

> *During my first and second years, I just went to meetings and helped arrange things. But my*

> *junior and senior years I coordinated Womenspeak (a month-long cultural celebration of women) and Students for Reproductive Freedom (a pro-choice group). One of the things that I liked about being involved in women's activities was that it was a great way to establish relationships with older students who became mentors. The Women's Center also became a safe place in what sometimes felt like a male-dominated community.*
>
> —ELIZABETH NEVINS, AMHERST COLLEGE

Most normal-sized colleges have activities and groups run by and for minority students. If you are a minority student, you probably will find yourself wondering early on if and how much you should become involved in minority student activities. Unfortunately, the answer is different for each individual. Here are some key questions to consider:

1. HOW IMPORTANT IS IT FOR YOU TO FEEL PART OF A LARGER GROUP?

The first year of college can be a difficult time of adjustment. Minority students, perhaps even more than other students, may feel alone or isolated, both in the classroom and in the residence halls. Affiliation with a minority group may provide you with a sense of belonging and make adjusting to the first year easier.

2. HOW MUCH TIME ARE YOU WILLING AND ABLE TO DEDICATE TO MINORITY ACTIVITIES?

Chances are, you will want to participate in numerous activities on campus, both minority and nonminority related. Belonging to several campus groups can be very time-consuming—group meetings are notoriously long. You need to consider time constraints when planning your level of commitment. Don't overburden yourself! One student's advice: "Don't be afraid to say 'no' if you don't have time to help organize an event or attend a meeting."

3. WHAT ARE THE POSSIBLE SOCIAL/POLITICAL IMPLICATIONS OF INVOLVEMENT AND HOW WILL YOU DEAL WITH THEM?

You should realize that group involvement may put you in some uncomfortable situations. For example, female students who become heavily involved with the women's center on campus often are surprised to find out that they are now labeled "radical feminists" merely because of this association. While labeling of this sort should not discourage your involvement, it is something to think about *before* becoming involved. If you choose to respond to other students who question your reasons for affiliation, honesty is usually your best weapon. Tell them exactly why it is important for you to be involved. Usually other students respond well to sincerity and honesty.

LIST OF MINORITY GROUPS/ACTIVITIES

Students of Color
- Student associations (e.g., Black Students Association)
- Cultural Centers
- Minority fraternities and sororities
- Community service projects that serve the local minority community
- Theme houses/residences
- Musical, theatrical, and dance groups related to cultural heritage
- Discussion groups covering minority issues

Women
- Women's Student Association
- Women's Center
- Community service projects for women like battered women's shelters, rape crisis hotlines, etc.
- Sororities and other all-female social groups
- Musical, theatrical, and dance groups related to women's issues

- Discussion groups covering women's issues
- Women's political action groups

Gay, Lesbian, Bisexual
- Student Center for gay, lesbian, and bisexual students
- Sexuality discussion groups
- Political action groups
- Social activities for members of the community
- Events celebrating alternative lifestyles

Students of Different Religions
- Religion-based student associations
- Fraternities or sororities
- Discussion groups covering religious issues
- Political action groups
- Theme houses/residences
- Eating clubs

SEEKING A BALANCE

Sometimes minority students (especially students of color and gay, lesbian, and bisexual students) feel both internal and external pressure to affiliate almost exclusively with their relevant minority community and, in the process, neglect connections with the mainstream, nonminority community. In the eyes of some in the minority community, a lack of total commitment is a sign of "selling out" or of being ashamed of your heritage, background, or sexual identity. As a minority student, you need to start thinking about how much of a commitment you are willing to make and how you will deal with students who question your level of commitment.

Remember that you are not playing an all-or-nothing game. You can affiliate with your relevant minority community and not totally disconnect yourself from the larger mainstream community. In seeking a balance, you may find a profound sense of belonging in the minority community, without losing the benefits of friends, organizations, and activities unrelated to your minority status.

SELF-SEGREGATION

Self-segregation can occur in class (sitting by other minority students), in the dining halls (eating at all-minority tables), and in the residences (choosing a minority roommate or living in a fraternity or sorority). Often students self-segregate without even realizing they are doing it. Of course, there is nothing wrong with self-segregation. Being with others like ourselves can help us to understand and define our identity and provide comfort during the often stressful college years.

The danger of self-segregation results from what is potentially lost from being with those unlike you. A large part of the college experience is meeting and getting to know a large variety of people. Self-segregation obviously has the potential to limit your ability to know and understand a wider spectrum of individuals. As you decide where you are going to live and who you will spend your time with, be cognizant of the advantages and disadvantages of self-segregation.

> *There is no such thing as self-segregation. And, if there is, discussion of it should not be confined to the behavior of minorities. Why are blacks and other minorities considered to be self-segregating when the majority group is doing the same thing in larger numbers? Perhaps minorities are viewed as self-segregating because they're easier to identify. In other words, it's easier to point out five members of a minority group sitting at a lunchroom table than to notice the 500 members of the majority group "self-segregating" in the rest of the cafeteria.*
>
> —CALVIN GLADNEY, CORNELL UNIVERSITY

DEALING WITH CONTROVERSIAL AND DIFFICULT ISSUES

> *A group of us were talking and a friend told an anti-Semitic joke. I am not even sure he realized his story was anti-Semitic. But I felt uncomfortable. I think everyone around me felt a little uncomfortable. I told him that, as a Jew, his remarks offended me. He actually thanked me for explaining my feelings. It's one thing hearing a minority person telling a joke about his or her particular minority group; it's quite another to hear the story from someone who is not a member of that group. I'm glad I said something.*
>
> —GLORIA BROWN, UNIVERSITY OF CALIFORNIA, BERKELEY

During your college years, be prepared to hear racist remarks on campus (and perhaps even in the classroom) and to see offensive literature. Sometimes a racist remark or offensive literature can precipitate a university-wide forum to discuss the issue of diversity on campus. Other times such events spark organized discussions within your minority community. In many cases, however, there will be no major outcry. You will need to decide how you want to address the situation by yourself or with a small group of peers. For example, you may be eating dinner with a group of friends and someone will say something that offends you. Realize that there is no "right" way to respond. Some people feel comfortable confronting the individual right there. Others prefer not to say anything and simply avoid that individual. Your reactions may change over time and may depend on the situation and your relationship with the individual in question.

Racist behavior based on hate, as opposed to misunderstanding, should not be tolerated. If you are deeply offended by what another student (or even a professor) has said, you should feel free to bring your concerns to the attention of older students, your advisor, or the relevant administrator at your college. Most schools treat such behavior very seriously. Don't try to solve the situation by yourself. Ask an older student or someone you trust for advice on how to handle the incident.

DIFFERENCES WITHIN YOUR MINORITY COMMUNITY

Like any other group of people, a minority group will have its tensions, differences, and divisions. Invariably, someone will fall into the minority, even in a minority group. For example, you may be a conservative in an African-American community that is traditionally liberal or a feminist in a minority group not known for progressive views about women. There is nothing wrong with having different views, but you may want to think about how you will respond to others who question your beliefs. Most students respect differences of opinion that are based on honest reflection and sincere conviction. You may even inspire discussion within your minority community about some of these differences. Constructive, and sometimes heated, discussion is part of what makes college a meaningful and worthwhile experience.

INTERSECTIONALITY

"Intersectionality" is the term modern scholars of ethnicity, gender, and sexual orientation use to describe the phenomenon of simultaneously being a member of multiple minority groups. In other words, many minority students find themselves at the "intersection" of different minority identities. For example, you may be an African-American female or an individual who is both Latino and gay.

If you are in this position, do not despair. Many universities have student groups at the various intersections of minority identities. For example, your school may have an organization for gay, lesbian, and bisexual students of color. Some minority communities have their own organizations that acknowledge the intersection of identity. For example, the African-American, Asian-American, and Latino communities may each have their own organizations for women or gay and lesbian students. Many university women's centers have organizations for lesbian and bisexual women.

In addition to these intersectional groups, you also have the option of associating with several different minority groups. For example, an African-American women who is bisexual might find herself working with her university's African-American theater organization, helping to organize the next gay, lesbian, and bisexual dance, and staffing the university's women's center. Once again, you are not playing an all-or-nothing game. If you are an intersectional minority, you should seek out the people, the organizations, and the activities that make you feel the most comfortable and that add the most joy and meaning to your life—regardless of the demographics.

MAKING AN ACADEMIC PURSUIT OUT OF YOUR MINORITY IDENTITY

> *Combining my study of English literature with a second major in the history of African-American music was one of the most personally and academically fulfilling things I ever did. I learned a lot about the place of music in African-American culture and the importance of African-American music to broader American culture.*
>
> —MARTINA STEWART, YALE UNIVERSITY

For many of you, college will be your first opportunity to choose classes and an academic major. It also will be the first time you will have access to classes that focus specifically on minority groups and the minority experience. Many universities have full programs and departments in African-American, Asian, Asian-American, Latino, Latin American, and women's studies. Some universities even have programs in Native American studies and gay, lesbian, and bisexual studies.

Any student can take classes in these areas. Minority students, however, may feel particularly drawn to these fields of study. Some minority students are so excited about the opportunity to learn more about their culture, history, and traditions that they choose to major in a type of minority studies. Other minority students shy away from concentrating in these areas, perhaps because they are not "traditional" areas of study.

If you are interested in minority studies, you should try a class early on to see if it wets your appetite. If it does, you might want consider majoring in that area or combining that interest with a more traditional field of study, such as history or biology. Many students focus a more traditional area of study around their interest in minority studies. For example, you could major in history with a concentration in African-American history. Other students choose to double major, sometimes in two drastically different areas, such as Latin American studies and biology. Double majoring is not easy. You may need to plan your course work carefully from the very beginning to graduate in four years.

A FINAL BIT OF ADVICE

During your college years, you will spend a lot of time thinking about who you are and who you want to become. As a minority student, you might want consider how your minority identity plays a role in shaping how you define yourself. As you make choices about what to study, who to live with, and who to spend time with, remember that this process of self-definition belongs to you and to you alone. Don't feel pressured to be who you think others in your minority community or in the wider, mainstream community want you to be. Be true to the only person you really need to answer to—yourself.

CHAPTER 13

Roommates

> I'm temporarily falling quite out of love with life, Boston University, and my roommate. Since we've been living with each other inseparably for two months, we're picking up each other's expressions, finishing each other's sentences, and arguing more and more. It's starting to get to me.
>
> Of late, the scenario is:
>
> "Can I borrow your computer?"
>
> "TAKE it!"
>
> "Why does everything offend you lately?"
>
> "I'm not offended. I'm trying to STUDY."
>
> "Why don't you go to the lounge?"
>
> "Because I want to study here."
>
> "Well, fine."
>
> "FINE!" (Door slams)
>
> Approximate time until next confrontation: Seven minutes. I still adore her, though. I guess I do . . . usually. I mean how couldn't you adore someone you eat, sleep, shower, study, and breathe with 24 hours a day?
>
> —SAMANTHA GREY, BOSTON UNIVERSITY

ROOMMATE RULES: EVERYDAY ETIQUETTE

Those with brothers or sisters know that living with peers takes compromise and effort. Multiply the factor by five when you throw two people from disparate backgrounds into the same room. Scary stuff! Or is it?

Instead of worrying about your future living partner, consider that he or she is as overwhelmed and unsure about college as you are. Both of you will come to college—labels and titles you bore in high school defunct—forced to face hundreds of new challenges. While no one will ever say you and your roommate have to be best friends, a congenial living situation makes freshman year easier—and more fun.

Here are a few rules of etiquette to help you along the way.

> *This is what I tell all my girls during orientation: A new roommate is just like having a sister, but this time you don't know her.*
>
> —RESIDENT ADVISOR SHIELA WILSON,
> BLOOMSBURGH UNIVERSITY

1. GET IN TOUCH BEFORE SCHOOL STARTS.

Confront your nervousness and curiosity by contacting your roommate before school. A phone call will serve as a stress-reducer and give you a chance to coordinate belongings. Who's bringing the stereo? What about the telephone and answering machine? Do you need two hair driers?

Hopefully, as you are arranging details, some common interests will surface. If you learn that he was the high school quarterback, while you were president of the Physics Club, don't panic. In a few weeks, you will enter school as two individuals with something very much in common . . . frosh status or, in simpler terms, no status.

 Psst . . . Many schools do not release roommate names before school. In this case, you just have to wait until you arrive at school.

2. DON'T JUMP TO CONCLUSIONS.

The first glimpse you will get of your roommate may be amidst a collage of parents, siblings, and suitcases—pure chaos. Hold back judgments. Saying good-bye to relatives can be sad or embarrassing, depending upon the person.

Don't catch First Impression Syndrome (FIS); it kills enough friendships already.

3. PRIORITIZE STUDY HOURS.

Much like fingerprints, everyone's study habits are different. If you need silence for studying while your roommate cannot comprehend calculus without The Grateful Dead, negotiate evenings that you will trade going to the library or study lounge.

Compromise! Ask for quiet hours after 9 P.M. or offer your walkman. Budget your time so you do not pull all-nighters that keep both of you awake.

4. NEGOTIATE EARLY . . . START WITH THE PHONE BILL.

Voice your concerns early. Do you have pet peeves? Do you hate people who leave toenail clippings on the floor? It's easier to listen and compromise in the beginning of the year than two months into the semester.

Start with the telephone bill. Since one person probably has agreed to have the bill charged to his or her name, discuss payment procedures for the other person involved. How do you want to be paid? Cash or check? Do you want the money before sending in the bill?

While you are at it, air other reservations you have. What would be your reaction to your roommate's friend calling at 2 A.M.? Do you hate people who don't take complete phone messages? Do you like onions but not olives on your pizza?

During sophomore year, my friend had a roommate who was about as tight as Cher's jeans. He would always squirm his way out of paying his equal share.

For example, when we would order from Domino's, he would always volunteer to pay the delivery man. There would be three of us, and he would ask us each for a five spot. The problem was, the pizza only cost 11 bucks. He would then chip in his one dollar and eat about half the pie.

With the phone bill, he would only add in his long-distance calls and never pay his part of the local charges. My friend, who had to pay the rest of the bill, wanted to kill the guy.

With beer, he was even worse. He would only pay about half of what we did and then finish off three-fourths of the case.

My friend felt too cheap to bring it up, so he never did. I didn't either. It bugged us the whole year.

In the end, I wish we would have confronted him early in the year and talked to him about how he could have been a better roommate and friend. Other than having a tight wallet, he actually was one of the cooler guys at school. I'm sure he could have been a much better roommate and friend had we simply told him he wasn't being fair and negotiated the problem when it first came up.

—BEAU BROWN, PIERCE COMMUNITY COLLEGE

5. RESPECT R.E.M. (NOT THE MUSIC GROUP!)

Any Don Quixote can tell you that messing with your roommate's sleep is the last—the very last—thing you want to do.

In simpler terms, don't bring your buddies in to watch David Letterman when your roommate is taking a siesta. Don't slam doors or drawers at 8:20 A.M. Don't type a term paper till dawn when you know your roommate needs shut-eye. Don't study at night with the overhead light on when a desk lamp will suffice.

> *Blessings on him who first invented sleep. It covers a man all over, thoughts and all, like a cloak. It is meat for the hungry, drink for the thirsty, heat for the cold, and cold for the hot. It makes the shepherd equal to the monarch, and the fool to the wise.*
>
> —MIGUEL DE CERVANTES, *Don Quixote*

6. LIMIT OVERNIGHT GUESTS.

Be as flexible as possible with this one.

If your roommate has guests from home or other universities, offer to spend the night in a neighbor's room. Of course, if the visitor is staying more than a few nights, explaining that he or she needs to bring a sleeping bag is more than acceptable.

If you are the one with guests, make sure not to take advantage of the room. It's not just "yours."

 Psst . . . Overnight guests of the opposite sex present a special problem. This topic, often raising moral issues, should be discussed immediately and openly. Respect each other's opinions and define policy clearly. Better to confront embarrassing situations before they arise rather than at 2 A.M. when you walk into a setting tailored for a Michelangelo painting.

7. DEFINE PROPERTY RIGHTS.

During my first semester, I had a 4 P.M. psychology class. At various times during the week, my roommate would get home from an earlier class and change into my clothes. To make matters worse, she then would scurry off to a happy hour somewhere on campus.

Later in the night, I would run into her at an ATO or SAE party. She would greet me with an alcohol-induced smile and say, "By the way, thanks for the outfit . . . you know how well this color goes with my eyes." The statement would come at about the same time some guy would bump into her and spill beer all over my sweater. I wanted to shoot her.

The thing is, I was paying for being glib and dishonest the first week of school when I said, "Oh sure, borrow anything . . . really, I don't mind." I never thought she would take me up on it—daily.

—JESSICA HALL, SYRACUSE UNIVERSITY

Most college students do not mind sharing umbrellas, lending a few tapes, or spotting for a movie. Monopolizing a wardrobe or another's pocketbook is a whole different ballgame.

While you and your sister may have traded sweaters like baseball cards, your roommate might cringe every time you venture toward her favorite cardigan.

Don't allow the simple niceties of asking before borrowing fade as you become more familiar with your roommate. Respect your roommate's right to say no.

Damaged items should be replaced immediately.

8. CLEANING: KEEP YOUR END OF THE BARGAIN.

Discovering an immaculate college dorm room in October and finding the Seattle Mariners baseball club in the World Series share similar odds in Las Vegas. The speed of light to one, to be exact!

If you are used to starched sheets, forget it. Learn to tolerate a roommate's unmade bed. But just because you are discarding delusions of *House Beautiful* does not mean you should accept or create conditions which are unhealthy and/or unlivable.

Most importantly, be considerate. Don't let your wet towel mold on top of your roommate's desk—or yours, for that matter. If he or she asks you to remove the stale tuna salad from the refrigerator, don't argue . . . do it!

Lead by example. If you want to live in unblemished paradise, clean your side of the room and hope your roommate follows suit. Occasionally, you can even start the job for the loafer.

9. EXPECT NORMAL TENSIONS.

Even the best roommate situations can turn ugly. When everything bugs you—the way she brushes her teeth, flosses, combs her hair, flirts, applies too much eyeliner, and tries on 17 different outfits checking for fat rolls on her 97-pound body—RELAX! Don't turn your roommate into a scapegoat or a permanent punching bag. No one wants you to take the place of mom.

Take disagreements or conflicts in stride and try to get away from the room for a while. Finally, be tolerant, especially if your roommate has had a bad day.

10. STOP RUMORS BY NOT STARTING THEM.

> It seemed wherever I went first semester, I heard private conversations among four or five girls who obsessively attacked vulnerable aspects of their roommates. They drew pictures, reminiscent of elementary school squabbles, and gossiped until silenced by the entrance of the innocent victim.
>
> They would say things like, "Every time her boyfriend calls, even if she is already asleep, she'll jump out of bed and rush to see him. She has no mind of her own."
>
> Meanwhile, the oblivious roommate only heard rumors and received unjustified glares.
>
> —KATIE SAPADIN, EMORY UNIVERSITY

Don't volunteer the details of your roommate's life to the rest of the dorm, fraternity, or sorority. Weekly floor meetings should not serve as a gossip central, where the main agenda item is who owes $50 for a 93-minute phone call to the boyfriend at home. Remember ... trust, once violated, is impossible to regain.

11. TAKE ADVANTAGE OF, NOT OFFENSE TO, YOUR ROOMMATE'S CHOICE OF CHUMS.

During the first week of college, roommates tend to cling together. As the year progresses and your circle of friends multiplies, however, you may choose to socialize less and less.

Neither of you is responsible for the other's social life; personality differences undoubtedly will cause you to prefer different friends.

Instead of resenting your roommate for his selection of buddies, take advantage of it. Through each other, you can gain greater access to a network of people, cultures, ideas, and opportunities. The acquaintances you make through your roommate can only add to your college experience.

 Psst . . . Roommates, like brothers or sisters, can become best friends—but they don't have to be. Aim for congeniality. If anything more develops, that's an extra bonus.

12. IF EVERYTHING ELSE FAILS, CALL IN A MEDIATOR.

You have begged your roommate to stop leaving underwear on the floor. You have discussed it calmly and not so calmly. War looks inevitable. There's nothing you can do about it. But wait! What's that in the sky? Look . . . it's a bird. No, it's a plane. It's . . . it's a mediator!

Don't be afraid to call in a dorm counselor or a trusted friend of both parties when you and your roommate face an unpleasant stalemate.

Vocalizing the problem with an outsider may help both of you deal with the dilemma in a more constructive and less personal way. The mediator often will see obvious solutions that may never cross a miffed mind.

If both of you are still unwilling to compromise, ask the mediator to make the decision for you. Of course, both sides will have to abide by the ruling, regardless of who gets the short end of the deal.

To some, I had the perfect roommate situation. We both studied a lot, were neat, had early morning classes, and could sleep with the light on. What more could you want? But what seemed perfect could hardly be called that. My roommate and I had a bland, almost businesslike relationship. The only way I could describe her to my family was "like a bug in your soup—she doesn't take up much room."

While I was constantly rambling on about my day or my classes, she would merely listen and never reciprocate with a similar anecdote. Eventually, I stopped rambling, and together we redefined the word "silence."

Our conversation upon returning from Winter Break consisted of:

"How was it?"

"Fine."

It wasn't until March that she felt comfortable enough with me to share stories. We learned more about each other in the final two months than we had all year. A little late perhaps, but we finally became friends.

—JESSICA HALL, SYRACUSE UNIVERSITY

13. ALLOW TIME TO DEVELOP A REAL FRIENDSHIP.

When befriending another, sharing part of yourself proves crucial to a genuine bond. Although you may enjoy eating meals together or studying as a pair, no real friendship can progress beyond small talk unless both participants open up. It takes some people more time to do this than others. Be patient.

Speak honestly about your experiences and accomplishments. False displays of grandeur are unnecessary and unwelcome. Just as important, be a good listener. It's no coincidence that listeners have more "true" friends than talkers.

14. BE YOURSELF.

You shouldn't try to change your roommate, and he or she shouldn't try to change you. Why? Because:

1. Individuality is something to be admired, not frowned upon

2. Changing people never works anyway

If you do nothing else throughout your college years, be yourself and allow others that right. This doesn't mean you shouldn't try to grow and become a better person. However, playing games and pretending to be "who you are not" only leads to unforeseen problems and low self-esteem. The odd thing is, more people will like you for who you are rather than for who you pretend to be.

Be yourself . . . it's not as corny as it sounds.

CHAPTER 14

Greek Versus Dorm Life

Going Greek was one of the best decisions I've made since coming to college.

Especially at a big school, it's often hard to find your place. You're on your own for the first time. You don't know anyone. You miss being around things that make you comfortable.

But the Greek system can make a big school so much smaller. It offers you a house full of friends that most likely will stay with you for the rest of your life. It gives you a renewed sense of comfort because you are around people who are like you and who have chosen you to be in their group. It doesn't take away from your studies either; in fact, it helped me because many of my sisters were in the same classes, and we studied together in groups.

Also, if you're talking about fun, the Greek system gives you an active social life, which no dormitory experience can hope to match.

—SUSAN YATES, WASHINGTON STATE UNIVERSITY

The Greek system is a big thing at my school, but I didn't think I needed it.

To me, the Greek system is a social crutch. It's for people who can't make it on their own. Greeks hang around people that are exactly alike.

But isn't that the antithesis of what college is supposed to be about? College is supposed to

> *be about meeting new people—people who*
> *you maybe didn't come into contact with dur-*
> *ing high school. It's a time to learn about new*
> *ideas. The Greek system won't provide that.*
>
> *The dorms, on the other hand, have allowed*
> *me to meet a wide variety of people, given me*
> *just enough partying, and provided a good*
> *study environment. For me, the choice was*
> *easy.*
>
> —BRIAN GRAHAM, LAFAYETTE COLLEGE

WHAT DID PLATO THINK?

Plato, one of the original Greeks, envisaged a society where justice was founded on moral absolutes. While today's Greek system falls slightly short of Plato's utopia, it still uses the same alphabet . . . as well as providing an excellent housing alternative for many college students.

However, most incoming students opt for school-sponsored dormitories and choose to live in dorms that are single-sex, coed by room, or coed by floor.

Although this chapter cannot pretend to make the choice between becoming Greek or staying in the dorms, it will illuminate the differences surrounding these two living arrangements. Below are the answers to the most common questions regarding Greek versus dormitory life.

SOME COMMON QUESTIONS

1. HOW DO HOUSING ARRANGEMENTS DIFFER?

Dorms Typical accommodations consist of two people sharing a room. Each dorm floor has one or two community bathrooms, depending on whether the floor is single-sex or coed. The typical dorm also may have a dining hall, television room, a mail room, study cubicles, a pay phone, and a laundry facility.

Greeks Most fraternities and sororities are based in large houses. Denoted by three letters of the Greek alphabet (e.g., Sigma Alpha Epsilon, Alpha Epsilon Pi), most Greek houses or "chapters" are located close to each other, sometimes on a street known as Greek Row.

As in the dorms, you may have to share a room. Even worse, many Greeks are forced to sleep on sleeping porches, which house about 30 students in one large room full of bunk beds. If you are sleeping on the porch, you may have to keep your clothes in another part of the house and commute back and forth.

Like the dormitories, Greek houses have dining halls, television rooms, mail rooms, study rooms, pay phones, a laundry facility, and a "party area" as well.

 Psst . . . Because of housing shortages, some colleges (e.g., UC-Berkeley) may require students to find off-campus housing, even during their freshman year. The housing office at your school usually has a list of apartments and homes available to students. One good reason to go Greek is that your fraternity or sorority undoubtedly will provide affordable housing.

2. WHAT ABOUT FOOD?

Dorms If you are on a school meal plan, count on eating two to three meals a day in a specified cafeteria. Some meal plans, however, allow you to dine in a variety of campus cafeterias, each with a different style of food (Mexican, Italian, etc.). Check out the meal options, paying special attention to the number of meals you are allotted and the stipulations on your plan. If you sign up to eat 20-plus meals a week, remember that you will have get up for every breakfast—and that's often when the roosters are crowing—and rarely have the option of eating out. Signing up for 14 meals a week may be more prudent.

Greeks Most Greek chapters have cooks who make all the meals. The quality of food, therefore, is contingent on the ability of the cook. Depending on the student, taste buds may play a slight role in determining which houses you rush.

3. DO LIVING COSTS DIFFER?

Dorms Although tuition fluctuates from college to college, housing costs remain relatively the same. Regardless of whether you are in a fraternity or dorm, expect to pay at least $1,500 per semester for room and board.

Greeks A common misconception is that Greeks pay more for housing because they have so many social functions. Fraternities and sororities are able to keep living costs low and still have a multitude of social gatherings because members perform many of the household chores otherwise taken care of by paid employees. Greeks often wash dishes, clean the bathrooms, and make physical repairs themselves.

4. WHAT IS THE PROCEDURE FOR JOINING?

Dorms You sign up, you pay, you're in. Actually, it's not quite that simple.

Many colleges allow you to request specific dorms. Ask upperclassmen from your hometown about the differences between the dormitories on campus. Some are better than others.

Many colleges also give you the opportunity to select coed, single-sex, all-freshmen, or four-class dormitories.

Greeks Joining a fraternity or sorority is slightly more complicated than signing up for a dormitory. Instead of choosing a place to live, a student must be invited to join the Greek system.

This invitation to join, called a "bid," must be approved by a large majority of the sorority or fraternity members. Bids are given out following a period called "rush." Although it may seem that the fraternities and sororities do most of the "choosing," this is certainly not the case. You, in effect, do most of the "choosing" by deciding which houses you wish to rush and which houses you wish to ignore.

Rush takes place during the summer at some schools; in this case, you might have "pledged" (or chosen to join) a fraternity or sorority before you even begin your freshman year. At other universities, rush takes place during the school year.

Various colleges handle rush differently. At many schools, the women go through formal rush and visit every sorority before deciding on which one they wish to pledge. Men, however, usually get to choose which fraternities they want to rush without looking at all the houses. Although you can join only one house, you can rush as many as you wish.

Those students who receive a bid to join a fraternity or sorority must go through a pledge period before they become members. During this pledge period, the pledges are expected to perform various tasks for the "actives," the members of the house. These tasks usually are given with good intentions. The pledges may be asked to clean dishes or rake the lawn. Sometimes, however, the tasks can be abusive; this is called "hazing." Hazing is illegal at all schools and fraternities and sororities can be severely punished for this type of pledging.

5. HOW DOES THE SOCIAL LIFE DIFFER?

Dorms You have a lot more control over your social life in the dormitories than you do as a Greek. Although your dormitory will undoubtedly throw parties and have meet-

> *During my first year of college before I transferred, I attended the University of Washington, a state school with a large, influential Greek system. At the beginning of the year I went through rush and joined the Tri-Delts. Although I lived at the sorority, I had several friends who lived in dorms and who were not socially affiliated with the Greek system.*
>
> *As I became more familiar with the social life of a dormie, I noticed it didn't seem much different from the social life of a Greek. Each held weekly meetings, threw parties, sponsored study breaks, and planned off-campus excursions.*
>
> *In spite of the similarities, a considerable number of dormies were adamantly opposed to the Greeks. We are talking total resentment—almost fanatical. Their criticism must have been directed toward something other than Greek social life because dorm social life was essentially the same.*
>
> —LESLIE FRIEND, UNIVERSITY OF CHICAGO

ings, your attendance at these events is never mandatory. The events are simply put on for those who wish to attend them.

In the simplest of terms, you make your own social life in the dorms. You can go to as many parties as you like or you can study until the Red Sea parts again.

Greeks It is much easier to have an active social life in the Greek system. There are more parties, more functions with other fraternities and/or sororities and, most importantly, a more "social" crowd. In addition, your attendance at many of these events is mandatory or, at least, strongly suggested.

Being in a fraternity or sorority also puts you in a more "social" scene. For example, it is quite common for a fraternity brother or sorority sister to set you up on a date with one of their Greek friends.

WHAT IS AN UNHOUSED FRATERNITY OR SORORITY?

Along with a housed Greek system, some campuses have unhoused fraternities and sororities. These unhoused Greeks hold meetings in a specified area on campus each week. Their members may live in the dorms or off campus.

Unhoused Greeks claim they have the best of both worlds. The students can intermix with the variety of men and women found in the dorms while still maintaining many of the bonds formed in a fraternity or sorority.

GREEKS VERSUS DORMS: ADVANTAGES AND DISADVANTAGES

I was ambivalent about joining a fraternity at first. Then I thought about it: Why am I going to college in the first place? Is it because of the degree? Partly . . . but I could get a degree at night school, if I was that desperate.

Is it because of the teachers? Partly . . . but teachers, no matter how good, certainly don't justify the huge amount of money I'm dishing out for tuition. So, why? Why am I going to college? I think the main reason for going to college is the other students you meet.

A fraternity, for all its negatives, is a great way to meet 50 new guys who, in a lot of ways, are a lot like you. My best friends are in my fraternity. And they will be my friends for the rest of my life.

No matter how you look at it: that's a whole bunch of guys who are going to be your business contacts, your tennis partners, your whatever-you-want-them-to-be. That's a big part of what college should be about.

—GREG GOTTESMAN, STANFORD UNIVERSITY

If you're not in the Greek system at a big school like the University of Washington, you basically have to work really hard just to have a social life.

—KATIE MACDONALD, UNIVERSITY OF WASHINGTON

I went through rush and pledged a sorority but found the whole thing to be too fake. After we were initiated as pledges, my newfound sisters immediately began crying and telling each other how they were all best friends now.

We were all holding these candles in a dark room and each girl would tell the whole group her deepest and darkest secrets. Then she would cry and thank everybody for letting her "bond" with the sorority. But I couldn't help thinking, "I don't even know these people and I'm supposed to tell them my deepest and darkest secrets."

For some, that's great but sorority life wasn't for me.

—PAM BROWN, SAN DIEGO STATE UNIVERSITY

> *Coming from out of state, I was apprehensive going to UCLA because I didn't really know anybody. Joining a fraternity gave me a place to belong.*
>
> —TIM ENG, UCLA

In a nutshell, a fraternity or sorority is going to give you a more active social life and a closer-knit group of friends. Your time will be more regimented, but most of the activities you participate in will be enjoyable. The most often heard complaint about Greeks is that they tend to be superficial, caring only about their fraternity and/or sorority and not about other things affecting the college community or the world.

A dormitory will allow you more freedom than a Greek house. You will live with a wider variety of people, including both men and women. The friends you make, however, probably will not be as long-lasting as those made in the Greek system, nor will you have the fellowship that the Greek system fosters.

TEN BASIC CONSIDERATIONS OF GREEK VERSUS DORM LIFE

As you have read, there are advantages and disadvantages to both Greek and dorm life. Below are 10 considerations that may help you to form a clearer opinion as to where you stand in the Greek versus dorm picture.

1. Greeks live in an all-male or an all-female environment. Dormitories can be co-ed. Which would you prefer?
   ☐ Greeks
   ☐ Dorms

2. Greeks usually do things together; their activities center around large groups. Those in the dorms do more things individually or in very small groups. Which would you prefer?
   - ☐ Greeks
   - ☐ Dorms

3. Greeks usually decide what activities and charities to support as a group. You are expected to back the group's decision. In a dorm, your decisions as to what you support will be mostly your own. Which would you prefer?
   - ☐ Greeks
   - ☐ Dorms

4. Greeks usually have their time more regimented. Greeks are expected to perform house duties and the like. In a dorm, your time will be less regimented. Which would you prefer?
   - ☐ Greeks
   - ☐ Dorms

5. Greeks tend to be homogeneous. They choose people who they think will fit in well with the group. This usually makes for a spirited environment. In the dorms, there are more people from different countries, religions, races and socio-economic backgrounds. Which would you prefer?
   - ☐ Greeks
   - ☐ Dorms

6. During the pledge period (usually one quarter), the Greeks demand a huge amount of time from their pledges. Although you undoubtedly will have fun, you may have to sacrifice some study time. The dorms have nothing like this. Which would you prefer?
   - ☐ Greeks
   - ☐ Dorms

7. If you plan on becoming a Greek, are you prepared to meet rejection? Many times you won't receive a bid from the house you wanted; it's possible that you may not

receive a bid from any house at all. The dorms have nothing like this. Which would you prefer?

☐ Greeks
☐ Dorms

8. In the Greek system, you will determine who you live with and actually vote on who you think should be in your house the upcoming year. In the dorms, you live with people who are randomly selected. Which would you prefer?

☐ Greeks
☐ Dorms

9. Greeks usually provide their members with an active social life. In the dorms, you are more individually responsible for your social life. Which would you prefer?

☐ Greeks
☐ Dorms

10. Greeks tend to keep their fraternal or sororital ties long after college is over. This may lead to business contacts or just friends in different areas of the country. Although you can make close friendships in the dorms, the long-lasting ties are usually harder to maintain. Which would you prefer?

☐ Greeks
☐ Dorms

THE BIG QUESTION: SHOULD YOU RUSH?

If you have any questions about whether or not you should rush, do it. You can always back out later.

Still, don't go into rush with your heart pinned to your sleeve. The rush process is not perfect. It favors the more outgoing and the more physically attractive. Actives make decisions on first impressions. The system is, at best, superficial. Keep this in mind and be prepared to face rejection.

> *I would encourage everyone to rush. Even if you are not planning on pledging a fraternity or sorority, rush is probably the best time you will have to meet people and make new friends.*
>
> *But be prepared to face rejection! I had a friend who was dying to be in the Greek system, but she was rejected by all four of the sororities that she wanted to get into. She was extremely hurt. It's hard not to take that sort of rejection personally.*
>
> —PAM BROWN, SAN DIEGO STATE UNIVERSITY

LAST BUT NOT LEAST: BE YOURSELF!

Regardless of whether you are rushing a fraternity or sorority or planning on living in the dorms, remember to be yourself.

A lot of people will rush a fraternity or sorority and act totally different than they otherwise would. For example, a guy may get drunk every night, even though he hates drinking. This only leads to problems later when the people in your fraternity or sorority expect you to act a certain way and you don't want to.

As previous chapters in this book have suggested, other students probably will like you more for who you are than who you pretend to be.

CHAPTER 15
Laundry and Ironing

LAUNDRY

Directions for washing:

1. *Fill cap to line for normal load.*
2. *For tough spots and stains, pour detergent directly on soiled areas and rub in.*
3. *For handwashing delicate fabrics, add a little detergent to each gallon of water, then add item(s). Soak briefly, wash gently, then rinse thoroughly.*

These washing instructions, delectable in their simplicity, could seemingly be followed by any "Neanderthal."

Ah, but judge not lest ye be judged.

In reality, laundry can be a most difficult endeavor, as witnessed by the foibles of one college freshman. This frosh learned the hard way one of life's most important lessons: Never put reds with anything even remotely white.

Here I was, content with my whites in one neat pile and my darks in another. So, I scrambled down to the washing machines in the dormitory basement and carefully put my whites in two of the machines and my darks in two others. I put in the correct amount of detergent as per the instructions on the box and deposited the required number of quarters.

As I walked back into my room upstairs, I was aghast to see that I had forgotten to wash my red Stanford sweatshirt. I grabbed it and ran

down to the basement. The machines with the darks were already too full. You usually end up with more darks because of blue jeans, towels and stuff. Feeling pretty confident that enough time remained in order to fully cleanse my sweatshirt, I threw it into one of the machines with white clothes. I was pretty sure the red on the sweatshirt would not bleed. I had already washed it twice before.

The rest is history. I have been wearing pink underwear, socks, T-shirts, and sleeping in pink sheets ever since.

Let me say one thing before parting. You can totally mess up a midterm in college. You can forget your coat at a frat party. You can even date your roommate's old sweetheart, if you're daring. But never, ever, wash your reds with your whites.

—GREG GOTTESMAN, STANFORD UNIVERSITY

THE 12 COMMANDMENTS

Hopefully, this story will save you from the pink reign many college students face in their freshman year. Of course, "not putting reds in with the whites" is only one of the many rules of laundering and ironing. To keep you out of trouble, *College Survival* has consulted a few laundromats, tailors and moms for a list of basic tenets. The 12 commandments read as follows:

1. READ THE LABELS ON YOUR CLOTHES.

Poor Katie MacDonald. During her freshman year at Washington, she was forced to send home her newly purchased—

and newly washed—ski sweater to her seven-year-old cousin. Alas, it was even too small for the seven-year-old, and it became the pride of Katie's dog, Mugger.

Dear Katie, she should have read the label, which would have succinctly told her that 100% wool sweaters are not machine washable (except for certain types which are tagged as "machine washable"). She could have done it by hand in cold water or sent it to the local cleaners.

You don't have to be a Katie. Thanks to the Federal Trade Commission (FTC), all garments must have care instructions. For example, the label inside a sweater must tell you if the garment is machine washable, 100% cotton, and so on.

When packing for college, consider easy care fabrics like 60/40 polyester/cotton. Be aware that, although 100% cotton and 100% wool are in vogue, they often require extra care.

2. MAKE SURE YOU HAVE ENOUGH QUARTERS BEFORE BEGINNING YOUR LOAD.

In high school, quarters are like any other medium of exchange; they are worth no more than two dimes and a nickle. In college, however, quarters assume monumental significance. Ryan Drant, a junior at Stanford University, used to maintain a "special" quarters cup. No one was allowed near it.

You're probably wondering why quarters are so sacred? . . . well, just about everything at college requires quarters. Soda pop for that "all-night" paper . . . candy and gum for that three-hour seminar . . . and, yes, washers and driers.

Don't be the hall beggar. When you go to the bank, remember to request a few rolls of quarters. Ask for them when you're at the grocery store. Bring some from home. And, heaven forbid, don't go down the three flights of stairs without several in hand. Driers and washers usually require two or three quarters apiece. Taking into account that you will be using about three washers and two driers per "usual 10-day" laundry load, 10 or more quarters should suffice. Not cheap!

3. CHECK YOUR POCKETS.

"I wish I had a dime for every dollar my mom found in my jeans before washing them." That was Aristotle, wasn't it?

There are some things that you do not want as sparkling clean as your everyday duds. Your wallet, for starters. Your syllabus from your first anthropology class. Your calculus assignment. A picture of your new girlfriend. Gum.

So, do what mom has done for years: Empty your pockets before washing. It only takes a second.

4. ALWAYS SEPARATE DARKS AND LIGHTS.

This commandment includes the all-important separation of reds and whites. If you thought we were going to beat this dead dog into the ground, you were pretty much on target. But in all seriousness, remember this rule. If you think some article of clothing is dark (and it might run), don't put it into the load with whites. For example, blue jeans and *colored* collegiate sweatshirts are *dark*. Believe it ... new Levi 501s have colored more underwear than Fruit of the Loom.

5. USE PRE-WASH ON "STUBBORN" STAINS.

No, most college freshman do not have a ready supply of pre-wash in their room. Then again, a good number of college freshman do not care that much about "stubborn" stains. So, this one is up to you. If you like your clothes the way they were meant to be worn (without spots), get a bottle of pre-wash for a few bucks. Spray your smudges with the pre-wash and throw the article in with the rest of your clothes.

6. SET THE MACHINE ON COLD OR WARM WATER TEMPERATURE—NOT HOT.

Most detergents today are made to work well in all water temperatures. According to most moms and professional launderers, however, the "hot water" setting on commercial machines should never be trusted. Not only will hot water aid your dark clothes in bleeding all over their lighter peers, but it also will play a role in shrinking a major part of your wardrobe.

Commercial machines are set differently than home ones. The "hot" setting on commercial machines may be akin to hell fire. Cold water is always safer.

7. NEVER OVERLOAD THE MACHINES.

Big mistake. Sure, it is not going to kill the machine if you put a few extra socks in—but don't add a few extra towels. Almost every freshman hears about one notorious washing machine explosion before the end of the first year. Spend the extra 50¢ or you might be swimming in it.

8. BE SURE TO READ THE INSTRUCTIONS ON THE DETERGENT BOX.

Make sure to read the instructions on how much detergent to add to the load. When in doubt, it is better to use too little rather than too much. Too much soap can leave film on your clothes. It also can irritate your skin. Usually instructions will tell you to add a cup of powdered detergent. If a measuring cup does not come with the box, buy one . . . it's a pain to play the how-much-detergent-equals-a-cup game each laundry session. You can use the cap to measure liquid detergents. Premeasured tablets and packets are easier to use than liquids or powders, but they cost more, too.

9. USE BLEACH WISELY AND, OF COURSE, ONLY WITH WHITES.

Bleach is the rich man's washing tool. In other words, you don't really need it. Granted, it makes your whites whiter, but many college freshman run out of bleach and never feel like spending the extra money to replace it. Nevertheless, it can be helpful when employed correctly. Use it only when washing white clothes. Also, remember to put it in the designated dispenser or to add it after the water has completely filled the machine. Roger, an owner of a laundromat in Seattle, warns, "Do not pour bleach directly onto your clothes or you might burn a hole right through them."

In addition, bleach—when overused—has a tendency to weaken the fibers in your clothes, causing many articles in your wardrobe to become hole-infested at a faster rate.

So, until huge holes in odd places come back in style, use bleach wisely.

10. TURN YOUR PATTERNED CLOTHES INSIDE-OUT BEFORE WASHING.

Ah, the mysteries of laundering!

After the end of their first quarter, many freshmen find the designs on their T-shirts fading. If they only knew what mothers across the nation have known for years . . . that is, turn your patterned garments inside-out. By doing this, colors stay intense and designs intact.

11. WATCH THE TIME TO AVOID THEFT.

Woe to the guy or gal who finds the kid in his calculus class wearing his favorite sweater. Indeed, theft is the favorite subject among many college students and also among local thieves.

When it comes to theft, the washing machines are just about the easiest prey around. College students tend to let their clothes sit for hours while they read that next chapter, watch the fourth quarter of Monday Night Football, kiss their new boyfriend 10 extra times, or catch up on a little shut-eye. Next thing you know . . . K-Mart here I come!

Many college students avoid theft by sitting in the laundry room and doing homework while their clothes wash and dry. For those impatient ones, setting a timer and making sure to pick up the clothes as soon as they are finished makes sense. Besides, leaving your clothes in the drier or washing machine after the time has expired is unfair to others wishing to use the machines.

You also should leave a laundry basket (with your name on it) on top of the washer or drier in question. Not only will this encourage your dormmates to put your clothes in a clean basket instead of on the dirty floor, but it also will facilitate carrying your clothes up two or three flights of stairs.

12. FOLD YOUR CLOTHES AS SOON AS THEY LEAVE THE DRIER.

This hint should allow you to bypass most ironing.

For some reason (unknown to science), wrinkles and the time immediately after clothes leave the drier are directly proportional. If you fold your clothes as soon as they leave the drier, you will be assured of fewer wrinkles and spiffy-looking duds. It only takes a few minutes and will save you hours of ironing.

IRONING

T.J. Burke, a freshman at the University of San Diego, claims the worst thing about freshman year was the "wrinkles"—not from stress, not from age, not from sun. "Nope!" T.J. said. "It was those darn laundry wrinkles."

T.J. admits he should have learned how to wield an iron. And after some research, T.J. gave us six helpful hints.

1. KEEP THE BOTTOM OF THE IRON CLEAN.

You have washed your shirt. Looks great. You iron it. Even better.

But wait! What are those spots doing on your perfect shirt?

Oops, the bottom of your iron must have been dirty. It could have been soil from your floor or starch build-up.

Just know that, during iron use, any debris on the bottom of the iron will become firmly implanted in your garment. So, keep the bottom clean. Tissue paper will work. If that does not solve your problem, many experts recommend cleaning your iron with a light grade of steel wool.

2. IRON ON TOP OF A TOWEL.

> *It seemed simple enough. I had some serious wrinkle build-up, so I went down the hall, borrowed an iron, and got to work. My blue-shag carpet seemed like a good place to set the shirt, so that's where I started to iron.*
>
> *It was one of my best shirts. I'm using the past tense for a reason, of course. When I picked up the shirt, I had implanted most of the carpet onto the back of it—blue-shag carpet! I guess it must have been the heat from the iron. I never could get out all the carpet, but the shirt worked great for one of those '70s dances. You work with what you have.*
>
> —ED MALAKOFF, BROWN UNIVERSITY

If you don't have a smooth, clean surface on which to iron, make sure to set down a towel, preferably a white one.

At college, you won't have room to store an ironing board. Improvise effectively. A clean desk with a few white towels covering it is probably your best bet.

3. LIGHTLY SPRAY YOUR CLOTHES WITH WATER, SIZING, OR SPRAY STARCH BEFORE IRONING.

Have you ever ironed a shirt for an hour? Have you ever ironed a shirt for an hour and still had those awful wrinkles staring you in the face?

Spray starch, for a just a few bucks, is a miracle. It will save you time and give your clothes that professionally "pressed" look. In addition, spray starch will give your clothes extra body.

Sizing, which is located next to spray starch in the grocery store, may be even better. Apparently, this fabric relaxant gives you all the benefits of spray starch without causing starch build-up.

If spray starch or sizing is not available, water will get out most of the creases; still, water will not give your clothes body or that "crisp" look.

Silks and certain delicate fabrics should not be sprayed with starch, sizing, or water. Take delicate fabrics to the cleaners. Pressing a formal dress is usually not a good idea . . . let the pros handle it.

4. USE A STEAM IRON, IF POSSIBLE.

A steam iron is your best bet. If you have a dry iron, however, use it on the medium setting—not on hot! The hot setting on a dry iron may stick to your fabric, scorch, and possibly melt it.

A steam iron, on the other hand, is more forgiving. Haruko Yaguchi, a tailor for the past 40 years, uses a steam iron on even the most expensive garments. She gives a word of caution: Some areas in the country have "hard" water. In these areas, fill your steam iron with distilled water. This will increase the longevity of your appliance and decrease the chance of residue building on the bottom of your machine.

5. IRON THE COLLAR AND CUFFS FIRST.

Thankfully, there is a method to this madness called iron-ing. If you do not want anemic-looking garments after three or four rounds of pressing, iron your shirts in this order: (1) the collar, (2) the cuffs, (3) the sleeves, (4) the back, and (5) the front. Of course, you should iron the most important part of your garment last.

Once you have mastered the shirt, you can apply this method in various forms to the rest of your wardrobe.

6. DON'T FORGET TO TURN OFF THE IRON WHEN NOT IN USE.

> *I was ironing one of my favorite shirts one day when the phone rang. Usually I'm careful about turning off the iron before I get into other things. But this time I forgot, to say the least.*
>
> *It was a long-distance call—an old friend from home. We started talking and one of my hands just kind of left the iron sitting on the shirt.*
>
> *Ten minutes later I looked down and the shirt had a six-inch hole in it. The iron burned right through the shirt.*
>
> *If it was a pair of jeans, I could have turned them into shorts. But, in this case, I would have been exposing something I usually like to keep hidden. I always remember to turn off the iron now.*
>
> —JESSICA WEINMAN, UC-SANTA BARBARA

This tip is self-explanatory. Irons are hot. Really hot. If you don't turn off your iron by mistake, chances are you will be calling the local fire department. So, it's simple: Don't forget.

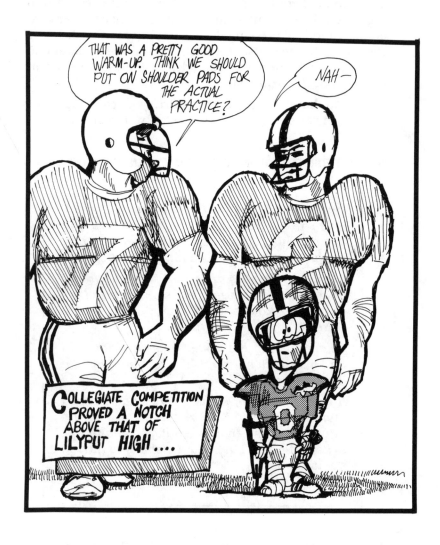

CHAPTER **16**

Athletics and Exercise: Varsity to Intramural

> *People always ask me how I can let varsity tennis take up so much of my time. They tell me how meaningless it is to hit a little yellow fuzzy thing over the net. "What about education? What about girls? What about fun?" they ask.*
>
> *"What about fun?" I respond. First, there is nothing I like better than a competitive three-set match in the heat of the day. Second, while others are relieving stress through unneeded Z's or hops and barley, I can always count on a good practice to ease my mind. Third, where education is concerned, I have this motto: "Strong mind, strong body." A healthy body allows you to concentrate harder and study more efficiently. Finally, as far as girls are concerned, they love guys in tennis shorts.*
>
> —KEITH VERNON, UNIVERSITY OF PUGET SOUND

SHOULD YOU PARTICIPATE?

If you ever played a sport in high school, if you ever got together with some friends for a game of two-hand touch, if you ever went jogging—get you yet?—heck, if you ever took a walk in a park, athletics and/or exercise should play some role in your collegiate experience. Anything is better than lethargy!

Even if you are not planning on playing a varsity sport, the least you should do is join an intramural team, jog, walk, or take an aerobics class. Exercising regularly contributes to better health and allows the mind to think more clearly.

WHAT SPORTS DO COLLEGES OFFER?

Colleges offer almost every sport imaginable on some level (e.g., varsity, club, intramural). Baseball. Basketball. Football. Tennis. Swimming. Soccer. Lacrosse. Wind surfing. Fencing. Tae Kwon Do. Chess?

If the school does not provide your desired sport, finding an interested group of guys and girls is never difficult, especially at larger schools.

WHAT ABOUT VARSITY SPORTS?

> *We had two individuals on our team who each played less than two years of high school soccer. They both walked-on. Neither was all-state or all-league in high school. Yet, they graduated as four-year starters on a women's soccer team that was ranked in the top five in the nation. Both of them were captains of the team. One of them was an All-American.*
>
> —COLLEEN HACKER, PACIFIC LUTHERAN UNIVERSITY
> SOCCER COACH

Comparing high school athletics to college athletics is like comparing a paper airplane to an F-15. Students who don't realize the difference are leaving the door open to disappointment.

Colleen Hacker, the women's soccer coach at Pacific Lutheran University, insists that students be realistic in assessing their athletic ability. "Simply being the star on your high school team does not guarantee success at the college level," she said.

Nevertheless, the high level of competition should not discourage those who are interested from trying out. Be realistic—but never sell yourself short.

How Do I Get Involved?

Sign-up procedures depend on your school. Varsity coaches have office hours; go in and speak with them if you are interested. Try-out times for the various varsity sports are easily accessible.

For intramural and club sports, most colleges have a recreation office where students can sign up. Dormitories and Greek houses often post sign-up lists as well. Some universities even give credit for those participating in school-sponsored sports—varsity to intramural. Talk about believing in the strong mind, strong body concept!

The Myths Surrounding College Athletics

Myths pervade college athletics. Recruiting and drug scandals fill newspaper headlines. Other stories of students graduating without knowing how to read or write warp the public's view of the true nature of college sports.

The next section will clear up three common myths.

Myth #1: YOU DON'T HAVE THE TIME TO PLAY.

Many freshmen heading off to college think they won't have time to breathe, let alone play a sport. Wrong!

The wonderful thing about college is that you will have more free time than ever before. Approximately three hours a day will be spent in class; the rest is yours. You are not going to study the entire other 21 hours, and, even with a part-time job, you still will have plenty of free time.

More explicitly, time should not be an excuse for abandoning exercise—at any level.

If you are a varsity NCAA Division I athlete (depending on the sport and season), expect to spend three to six hours a day. For example, during football season, Division I teams demand about six hours, including time on the field and in the training room.

Division II, Division III and NAIA athletes spend less time on the field. During each athlete's respective season, two to four hours is standard. In these divisions, more emphasis is placed on academic as opposed to athletic success.

Myth #2: THE ONLY "REAL" COMPETITION TAKES PLACE IN DIVISION I.

When one thinks of college sports, Division I teams like Oklahoma, Notre Dame, UCLA, Texas and Penn State come to mind. Why shouldn't they? When was the last time you saw Bates and Bowdoin on national television? Yet, while it is true that Division I teams get the press, serious competition takes place at all levels, from Division I to the NAIA.

Although Division II teams do not contend at the same level as Division I, it provides intense competition for even the best high school athletes. Many Division II athletes were

> *The only teams I ever watched during high school were the best in the country in their respective sports. Sure, it would be fun to play with the best, but, for me, playing is the most important thing. I never thought there would be such great competition and organization at a non-Division I school like Skidmore.*
>
> —MATT GALVIN, SKIDMORE COLLEGE

high school stars who wanted to play consistently for smaller schools.

Division III is different from Division I, Division II, and the NAIA in that it does not allow schools to provide athletic scholarships. Surprisingly, the level of competition, although somewhat less intense, remains high.

> *I was surprised to find competitive swimmers at the Division III level. But what surprised me the most was the degree of seriousness that existed at a small, liberal-arts school in everything from the scheduling to the coaching.*
>
> —SHELLEY FARMER, VASSAR COLLEGE

Less well-known than the NCAA, the NAIA has adopted different recruiting policies, eligibility requirements, and scholarship strategies. In terms of competition, the NAIA sits on the same level as Division II or Division III in the NCAA ranks.

> *I thought that NAIA schools were not competitive enough to be in the NCAA. I was dead wrong. They are quite competitive on the field and extremely serious about practice time.*
>
> —KEITH VERNON, UNIVERSITY OF PUGET SOUND

Myth #3: COLLEGE ATHLETICS HINDER ACADEMICS.

Headline: Basketball Star Joe Dokes Can't Read; Sues Former School.

Heard the story? Although these situations exist, they represent an exception to the rule. The majority of college athletes do not see athletics as detracting in any serious way from their academic pursuits. In fact, after questioning numerous college athletes, the consensus was that most received their *best* grades during the semester of their sport. Why? The athletes felt that having a sport to play forced them to balance their time and study more effectively.

> *Competing in a varsity sport added some needed discipline to my day. If I was not out hitting the tennis ball, I would have just played around and wasted time anyway.*
>
> —GEOFF TABIN,
> FORMER CAPTAIN YALE UNIVERSITY TENNIS TEAM

Still, the majority of student-athletes feel that it is best to take a "lighter load" during the season in which they play a sport. Why overburden yourself with academic units when you already have a huge athletic commitment?

GO FOR IT BUT WATCH THE ELBOWS!

"Show me a good loser and I'll show you a loser."

—LEO DUROCHER

Sure, everyone wants to win, but when playing club and intramural sports, remember that the same guys you elbow under the hoop are going to be sitting next to you in calculus class. So, take it easy unless you plan on studying differential integrals all by your lonesome.

In summary, go ahead and hit the three-pointers but be careful with those elbows.

BUT WHAT ABOUT WHAT MR. HUTCHINS SAID?

When I feel a desire to exercise, I lie down till it goes away.

—ROBERT M. HUTCHINS (1935)

Ah, Bob was a wimp.

CHAPTER **17**

Dating

> *All fall quarter I was dying to go on a date. Besides Nietzsche, that's practically all I thought about. The only problem was, I was too afraid to ask any women out.*
>
> *I was terrified of rejection. What if she said no? What if she told all her friends how much of a nerd I was? And then they told their friends and so on and so on and so on. Pretty soon, the whole school would know.*
>
> *So, instead of asking anyone out, I sat around thinking about Nietzsche some more. I hate Nietzsche. Meanwhile, my roommate was telling me I was a candidate for Dr. Ruth.*
>
> *Finally, I did it. I asked out a girl in my economics class. She said yes. She didn't think I was a nerd. She didn't tell any of her friends. We went out for pizza and a movie.*
>
> *And, you know something, I had a great time. Asking her out wasn't such a big deal after all.*
>
> —GREG GOTTESMAN, STANFORD UNIVERSITY

DATING: THE ANXIETY FACTOR

Without a doubt, this is the most anxiety-provoking chapter in *College Survival*. Regardless of whether you are new to the scene or an old pro, dating brings illusions of pride lost, time wasted, and hearts broken. No one—no matter how attractive—is completely comfortable with the idea.

But the truth is, learning how to deal with members of the opposite sex is one of the most important skills you will learn at college. You should date, you will date, and you'll have fun doing it!

Below are some answers to the most commonly asked questions about dating at college. Later in the chapter, *College Survival* will provide some helpful tips for your next date.

SOME COMMON DATING QUESTIONS

1. WHAT ARE SOME EASY WAYS TO BREAK INTO THE DATING SCENE?

You will arrive at college without any of the titles or labels you bore in high school. Your old group of friends will have dispersed across the country. Now what do you do?

For starters, talk to people. Talk to anyone and everyone, in your dorm, Greek house, or wherever. Visit some of the people you met in your classes. Besides being the best way to make friends, this is also an excellent way to meet potential dates.

In terms of an actual one-on-one date, fraternity and sorority formals and even dormitory dances will provide you with a golden opportunity to ask someone out.

Remember . . . you don't have to know a person that well to go on a date with him or her. It's freshman year. No one knows anyone that well.

2. WHICH IS BETTER: THE GROUP DATE OR THE INDIVIDUAL DATE?

To ease the anxiety of an initial date, many freshmen opt for a group date. When you are double-dating (or have hooked up with a group of friends with no one in particular as your date), interaction becomes much less intimidating. In fact,

> *For me, group dating is much easier, particularly when you're first getting to know someone. When there's other people to talk to, it's easier to relax and to have a good time.*
>
> *When you're on your first date, it's hard enough to find something to talk about—especially for five hours.*
>
> *You'll have plenty of time to get to know someone—if he's really someone you want to get to know. In the meantime, group dating is usually a more fun and a more relaxed way to meet someone.*
>
> —KRISTEN WHYTE, UNIVERSITY OF WASHINGTON

at many schools, group dating has become the preferred mode.

What group dates provide in liveliness and comfort, however, they often lack in intimacy. If you excel at one-on-one interaction or if you really want to get to know someone, the group thing might cramp your style.

Many students start out by group dating and, once they get to know someone well, ask that person out on an individual date.

3. WHAT ABOUT THE GIRLFRIEND OR BOYFRIEND YOU LEFT AT HOME?

Many freshmen come to school missing an extra piece of luggage, mainly in the form of a boyfriend or girlfriend at home. Sometimes these long-distance relationships are able to weather the pressures of maturity and huge telephone bills, but, more often than not, they fail.

It is usually a good policy to date other people at college. If you are calling your long-distance sweetheart everyday,

> *During my freshman year at Pomona, I was still going out with my girlfriend from high school. She was going to college two hours away, and we spent a lot of time commuting back and forth.*
>
> *While at that time that was the only decision I could make, I later realized that I had missed out on making a lot of new relationships and in getting involved on my campus.*
>
> *When your heart and mind are at another place, you pass up on many of the experiences of freshman year.*
>
> —DAVID MUSCATEL, POMONA COLLEGE

chances are you will miss out on many new experiences and some invaluable opportunities for growth.

Even if you plan on being loyal to your boyfriend or girlfriend at home, figure out some way to have an active social life. In this case, finding a group of close friends may be your best bet.

Finally, don't become paranoid about losing your hometown boyfriend or girlfriend. If it's meant to be, you have nothing to worry about.

4. WHAT ABOUT SEX?

Some freshmen drown themselves in their newfound freedom. Out of the clutches of mom and dad, they feel like college is a time to experiment, a time to let it all hang out.

Whether or not you have sex at college is completely up to you. But don't get too carried away with your own freedom. When it comes to sex, be careful and be choosy. Just because people around you are doing it—and there will be

> *My mother's advice to me before I left for college: Never trust a man. And, boys, keep your pants zipped.*
>
> —MOLLY PENNY, SANTA CLARA UNIVERSITY

plenty, perhaps even your roommate—doesn't necessarily mean you have to.

FOUR TIPS ON SUCCESSFUL DATING

There's nothing worse than a bad date. And you'll know when it's happening. Minutes will seem like hours, hours like days. Your stomach will turn. You'll start getting paranoid and anxious.

Ah, but never fear, *College Survival* to the rescue! While these next few tips cannot guarantee physical attraction, they should make your next date a little more interesting and definitely more enjoyable.

1. GO FOR IT!

One of the saddest realities about college is that students talk about dating more than they actually do it. People get caught up in the what-if-she-says-no or the what-if-he-doesn't-like-me game.

What students forget is that their classmates want to go out just as much as they do. Everyone wants to meet new people. Dating, although embarrassing at times, is a great way to do just that.

The problem with the next four tips is that, if you don't follow this first suggestion, the rest are moot. And, yes, it does take guts to ask someone out. But as Sir William Schwenck

Gilbert once said, "Nothing ventured, nothing gained." Take a chance.

2. BE FUN AND CREATIVE.

When planning your dates, try to be creative. Dinner at your campus cafeteria may be practical, but it's certainly not going to win over any hearts.

Be a little different, if you can. Here are a few sure-fire suggestions:

Date Suggestions:

1. Picnic . . . romantic, practical, perfect
2. Local comedy show . . . laughs galore, great icebreaker
3. Major sporting event . . . expensive but fun
4. Hiking . . . romantic but sweaty
5. Bicycling to a restaurant . . . athletic, fun, romantic

If the creative juices just aren't flowing, don't fret. The pizza–movie date is always a great alternative.

 Psst . . . A lot of students like to stay on campus for their first date. It's practical and casual. Besides, most freshmen don't have cars, and campuses are loaded with things to do. Concerts, lectures, movies, plays, sporting events, pizza parlors, coffee shops . . . many a relationship has been started over a cup of cappuccino.

3. LISTEN.

One of the strange paradoxes of life is that people love talking about themselves, but very few people love listening to people who talk about themselves.

Instead of talking about yourself, ask your date lots of questions. The way to a person's heart is to have him or her know you care.

If you like the person, you'll have plenty of time to shine and to wax philosophically. In the meantime, listen up. Your date will think you're one in a million, which you will be.

I had a friend who was dying to go out with this guy. He was handsome and seemed like he had a great personality. When he finally asked her out, she was practically counting down the days until the date.

But the date itself was a complete disaster. The handsome guy turned out to be the most self-inflated, self-important, self-loving human being on the planet. All he talked about was himself—in the car, at dinner, everywhere. My friend barely even got a word in. To say that she couldn't stand this guy is an understatement.

By the end of the night, she was sick—literally. She wanted to leave the date so badly that she started dry-heaving. It was the saddest thing I'd ever seen.

All I can say is that if you think talking about yourself is going to impress someone, think again. Listening works better.

—LESLIE FRIEND, UNIVERSITY OF CHICAGO

4. WATCH OUT FOR SCAMMERS.

By the time most freshman women reach their sophomore year, they've heard as many pick-up lines as Kim Basinger. College is home to many a scammer.

But, in all seriousness, beware of guys that are more physical than you would like or that try to entice you to do things you don't want to do.

Date rape is an ominous reality on most college campuses. Always use good common sense and be careful. If you are feeling uncomfortable, don't be afraid to leave. At the very least, state your intentions clearly.

Chapter 21, Campus Safety, covers this topic more extensively.

My mother always told me: Beware of guys with wandering eyes. But the truth is, you have to beware of more than that. Guys that ask you to go up and look at their fish tank . . . definite no-no. Guys that claim that they're related to someone famous . . . maybe, probably not. Guys that want to go for a walk but actually want to trek through the forest . . . later. Guys that emanate an odor which can be detected for a 10-mile radius . . . think again.

Seriously, be picky. There's a lot of great guys at college but there's also a lot of iffy ones.

—KIM BENAROYA, UC-SANTA BARBARA

CHAPTER **18**
Partying and Alcohol

My friends and I had set out on a quest: to seek and consume as much alcohol as humanly possible. With my girlfriend at my side, I had an added incentive. I wanted to prove to her that I could drink like the god I was (or thought I was).

The first four beers were easy. They went down cold and smooth. But, two beers later, I realized that my balance was shot. Besides that, all the women looked attractive, even the ones who weren't so great an hour ago. Beer goggles, yes!

Undaunted, I plowed through four more beers. I didn't even taste them. Then I danced and stumbled my way through an additional two and left the party at 1 A.M. By now, I was drunk. I had all the signs: blurred vision, slurred speech and a complete lack of balance. But, hey, I was a drinking deity! Right?

I returned to my friend's room only to find a bottle of vodka being passed around. After two shots, my personal time-space continuum went bad. The next thing I know, I am kissing this woman (not my girlfriend) and, a little later, throwing up in the toilet.

Yes, I had become a fallen god. I was sick.

And to make matters worse, my roommate's parents showed up at the door at 9 A.M. the next morning.

What did I learn? I learned that drinking 12 beers and then doing vodka shots is akin to hitting yourself over the head with a baseball

> *bat. I learned that the actual act of getting sick is nothing any god would want to play any part in. And I learned that everyone has a limit as to how much they can drink. On that night, I surpassed mine.*
>
> —BRYAN COHEN, CLAREMONT MCKENNA COLLEGE

PARTYING AND ALCOHOL: THE REALITIES OF COLLEGE

Partying at college is kind of like The Blob. You can't escape it. It will be a part of your life, regardless of where you go to school.

But while parties are part of the social scene at every college, the types of parties will differ with each school. At smaller, private schools, for example, the party scene may consist of gatherings of around 20 or 30 with alcohol and rowdiness at a minimum. At large "party" schools like Chico State or Arizona State, however, you may find scenes befitting the movie, *Animal House.* Everyday.

One thing will be the same at every party at every school: alcohol. Regardless of whether your campus is dry (alcohol is not allowed) or wet, you will have to make some tough decisions concerning alcohol consumption.

While *College Survival* does not condone or condemn drinking, it realizes that alcohol will play some role in your college life. Below are five tips to help you deal with two of college's biggest realities: partying and alcohol.

 Psst . . . Some of you probably are wondering why other recreational drugs are not covered extensively in this or other chapters. The truth is, drugs are "out" on most college campuses. This is not to say that people don't use them but that alcohol is the drug of choice at this time. Still, all of these tips can be applied to other drugs.

FIVE PARTYING AND ALCOHOL TIPS

1. KNOW YOUR LIMIT.

> *I was at a punk rock theme party and, believe me, I was playing the part. Chains surrounded my body. Handcuffs dangled from my small black mini-skirt.*
>
> *Before long, I found my way to the upside-down marguerita room and positioned myself for maximum consumption. In the next hour, I must have drunk around 10 upside-down margueritas. Feeling social and unaware of the nature of tequila, I then poured down a truckload of tequila poppers. Soon enough, the alcohol hit, and I found myself hugging the cool porcelain.*
>
> *I awoke the next morning at 5 A.M. surrounded by chains and handcuffs. I decided to make the trek back to my room and, if things hadn't been bad enough, the wind outside resembled a typhoon somewhere in the Philippines.*
>
> *So, here I was . . . freezing, hung over, and swearing that the next time I would know my limit.*
>
> —TINA SANTOS, UNIVERSITY OF PUGET SOUND

Whether it's peer pressure or just plain thirst, it's very likely you will try drinking alcohol at college. If you drink too much, count on getting sick. Really sick. Although people have different tolerance levels, four beers or the equivalent in hard liquor is usually enough to cause damage—to your brain cells, if nothing else.

Psst ... Here's an equation you might want to commit to memory:

1 beer = 1 glass of wine = 1 shot of hard liquor

2. DON'T WEAR NICE CLOTHES.

> *I had just gotten a new brown suede jacket and wanted to wear it to the big party that night. But about half way through the evening, some guy spilled jungle punch all over my jacket. It took a trip to the dry cleaners and a few twenties to get the stain out.*
>
> *Next time I'll leave the new stuff at home and party in the stuff I don't care so much about.*
>
> —JILL TACHER, UC-SANTA BARBARA

Here's a little *College Survival* addendum to **Murphy's Law:** The chance of someone spilling a drink on you is directly proportional to the cost of your clothes.

Nice clothes and shoes are magnets for any item that stains permanently. This doesn't mean you should dress like a slob when going to a party, but avoid wearing your best duds.

Remember that alcohol affects balance.

3. DON'T DRINK AND DRIVE.

Eloquence isn't needed here: Drinking and driving is just plain dumb. Besides, there's no excuse for it. Many alternatives exist. For example, many students have started assigning a "designated driver," a person who does not drink and is responsible for transportation to and from a party with alcohol.

I met Neil, Adam, and James the first day I arrived at Georgetown. We became friends and started trekking to all the big parties to drink and experience the joys of freshman year.

Three weeks into school, we climbed into Neil's old Ford Thunderbird and took off with a half gallon of rum and a case of beer to crash a party at the yacht club on the Potomac. After many hours of drinking from a fully stocked bar, I headed back to the car. With a very drunk Neil at the wheel, we somehow made it back to the university parking lot, only then to wreck four cars while trying to pull into a parking space at 30 miles per hour.

Neil was arrested. Adam, James and I were just warned by the Adjudication Board, and the incident was recorded on our disciplinary record. After that, I stayed away from my new friends. When I look back upon it, I see an insecure freshman who desperately needed friends and who almost risked his life because of it. Now I have many close friends at college . . . Neil, James, and Adam are not among them.

—MATT CARR, GEORGETOWN UNIVERSITY

College campuses are into the act as well, offering "saferide" programs. This service, which is usually free, allows students to call at any time from any place to receive a "safe" ride home.

Taxis and buses are other options. Besides that, you can always spend the night at the party's locale. Classmates usually don't mind you crashing on their couch or floor, especially if you're too drunk to drive.

4. DON'T BELIEVE EVERYTHING YOU HEAR.

Beer before liquor/never been sicker.

Liquor before beer/have no fear.

—UNKNOWN

Ah, the infamous college saying. But according to most doctors, this oft-repeated adage holds little truth.

What matters is how much you drink, not what type or in what order. Don't drink 10 shots of hard liquor before having a few beers just because you heard it won't make you sick. It will.

5. FIND A BALANCE BETWEEN PARTYING AND ACADEMICS.

I took chemistry in college, expecting the same results I got in high school. The only problem is, I partied until the night before the first midterm and bombed the test. Needless to say, my grade was closer to the right end of the alphabet than the left.

After that, I realized that partying at college is fine, but you have to keep it in perspective. I set some limits for myself, and my transcript thanked me for it from then on.

—BETTY BAUGH HARRISON,
UNIVERSITY OF NORTH CAROLINA

Finding a balance between socializing and academics is integral to college success. Too much partying and you may find yourself on academic probation.

Don't let the brainiacs who get straight A's and party five nights a week fool you. Besides, your tuition check is supposed to go toward an education, not Miller Lite.

To paraphrase Aristotle, quite a wine drinker himself: "Virtue comes from following a course of action somewhere between the extreme of too much and that of too little."

CHAPTER 19

Get Ready To Be Sick: Medical, Dental, and Psychological

> *During winter quarter, I was plagued by a nagging cold. Even though I felt lousy, I didn't want to cut down on my activity load. I had just joined a fraternity, was involved in intramurals, wanted to keep up my grades, not to mention getting to know that girl in my economics class a little better.*
>
> *When the cold didn't go away and I started running a high fever, I realized I needed to take it easy. One of my friends played nurse, and I drank more OJ than Simpson.*
>
> *Two weeks later, I ended up at home, missing two weeks of school with mononucleosis.*
>
> *Next time, I won't play doctor . . . I'll go to one.*
>
> —DAVID MUSCATEL, POMONA COLLEGE

PREVENTIVE MEDICINE

Everyone should practice preventive medicine; indeed, the best cure for ailments is not getting them in the first place. At the very least, heed these three pieces of advice:

1. Get adequate sleep
2. Maintain a well-balanced diet
3. Stay away from others who are sick

Obviously, circumstances such as finals and weekend parties will prevent perfect observance of these three commandments. But follow them whenever possible.

WHERE SHOULD YOU LOOK FOR MORE INFORMATION?

Be careful [when] reading health books. You may die of a misprint.

—MARK TWAIN

Symptoms and treatments for upper respiratory illnesses, gastrointestinal problems, sexually transmitted diseases, and other common ailments are mentioned below. For more information on the following illnesses, consult *The Campus Health Guide* by Carol L. Otis, M.D. and Roger Goldingay.

UPPER RESPIRATORY INFECTIONS

BRONCHITIS AND PNEUMONIA

If you have been coughing severely for five or six days, have chest pain, and/or shortness of breath, you may have bronchitis, an infection of the respiratory tubes. Even worse, you could have pneumonia, an infection of the lungs. Go to the doctor immediately.

THE COMMON COLD

Infamous signals of the common cold include a runny nose, sneezing, watery eyes, and sinus congestion. While antihistamines can help the sinuses and Tylenol the aches and pains, nothing works better than pumping fluids and taking in some extra shut-eye.

 Psst ... Most cold medicines contain antihistamines, which can cause drowsiness—not so great if you have a mid-term in the morning! Cough suppressants also can make you drowsy as they may contain significant amounts of alcohol (Nyquil is 50 proof!). Ask the pharmacist for medicines that will not make you fall asleep (e.g., Sudafed for the sinuses and runny nose and Robitussin for the cough).

THE FLU

Do you have chills? What about aches, pains, and a high fever? Watch out! You may have the flu.

Acetominophen (e.g., Tylenol) will be most effective against the fever, chills, aches, and headaches, while an over-the-counter cough suppressant can lessen a harsh cough.

As with colds, however, rest and fluids will work better than any drug.

Doctors suggest not taking aspirin to relieve flu and cold symptoms because of its recent connection with Reyes Syndrome. Reyes Syndrome involves liver and kidney failure and has been linked to aspirin—when used to combat viral illnesses.

MONONUCLEOSIS

The infamous "kissing disease," which can be spread through direct contact, starts with chills, a fever, a sore throat, and swollen glands.

The most conspicuous signal, however, is fatigue. If you feel unusually tired for a more than a few days, you may have mononucleosis. Do not pass "Go." Do not collect $200. See a doctor immediately.

STREP THROAT

This treatable bacterial infection is characterized by a nasty sore throat and fever. Caused by the *Streptococcus* bacteria, strep throat may be indistinguishable from a common viral sore throat. Untreated, strep can lead to complications including rheumatic fever and kidney problems. See a doctor for a throat culture if your symptoms persist longer than two days.

GASTROINTESTINAL PROBLEMS

HEPATITIS

Symptoms of this serious disease include weakness, loss of appetite, nausea, vomiting, dark brown urine, and jaundice, a yellowish discoloration of the skin and tissues.

If you think you have hepatitis, seek medical attention immediately.

STOMACH ACHES AND DIARRHEA

Most students choose greasy fast foods over balanced meals. This type of chaotic diet leads to stomach problems. Products like Kaopectate and Imodium A-D help diarrhea, while Tums and Rolaids can relieve an upset stomach. But don't fool yourself. Eating sensibly works best.

 Psst . . . Don't take aspirin for a stomach ache. It can be a stomach irritant!

SEXUALLY TRANSMITTED DISEASES (STDs)

Most students possess an "I'll never get it" attitude about sexually transmitted diseases (STDs). Don't ask for trouble. Take preventive measures like using a condom.

If you have had intercourse with a person who is found or is suspected to have an STD, see a physician or go to an STD clinic immediately. The embarrassment is worth avoiding later complications.

If you have an STD, you should tell your partner(s) so that he or she may be checked as well. Even though it may be difficult to confront your partner, he or she deserves not to be put through any unnecessary complications due to your delay.

 Psst . . . If you are sexually active, make sure contraceptive devices are easily accessible. Don't assume your partner has taken the necessary precautions. And, remember, oral contraceptives do not protect against STDs.

AIDS

The most recent studies suggest that one in every 1,000 college students has the AIDS virus; but according to many reports, the figure is even higher. This disease is predominantly transmitted through intercourse or the sharing of contaminated needles. AIDS kills. There is no cure at this time.

Be careful. Wear a condom. Don't share needles. Better yet, stay away from drugs altogether. Your life may depend on it.

CHLAMYDIA

Chlamydia, an infection in the vagina or urethra, is characterized by burning and frequency of urination. A bacterial STD, chlamydia is treatable with antibiotics. See a physician. Your partner, even if he or she is showing no signs of the disease, should be treated simultaneously.

GONORRHEA

Gonorrhea, caused by a bacteria called *Neisseria Gonococcus*, is characterized in men by painful discharge or burning during urination. In women, no symptoms usually occur until the Fallopian tubes and ovaries are infected. This leads to what is commonly called Pelvic Inflammatory Disease or PID. Severe abdominal pain, a fever, and chills are hallmarks of PID. If you think you may have contracted gonorrhea, see a doctor immediately.

HERPES

Herpes, a viral STD, produces blisters on the penis or labia and the mucous membranes. The moderately painful sores caused by herpes viruses usually dry up and disappear in about two weeks. Once contracted, herpes cannot be cured, and the herpes virus may keep reactivating. If you think you might have contracted herpes, seek medical attention. Some antiviral prescription medications (e.g., Zovirax) may alleviate the severity of an outbreak.

SYPHILIS

This now rare venereal disease begins with the formation of a relatively painless sore or ulceration in the genital region. If you see sores in these areas of your body, seek medical help as soon as possible. Once the sores go away, you still may have the disease but the diagnosis will be much harder to make.

WARTS

Warts or condylomata, infections caused by the papilloma virus, start as small flesh-colored growths. They are usually painless but will multiply throughout the genital region if not treated. Condylomata are associated with cancer of the cervix in women. If you see these infections, see a physician immediately.

MISCELLANEOUS AILMENTS

It's no longer a question of staying healthy. It's a question of finding a sickness you like.

—JACKIE MASON

ACNE

Welcome to Acne, Part II: The College Years. Contrary to popular belief, food and drinks like chocolate, nuts, root beer, and Coca-Cola do not directly cause acne. Nevertheless, they may increase the severity of an outbreak. Over-the-counter products that contain benzoyl peroxide, sulfur, resorcinol, and salicylic acid work well. Still, no better prevention exists than gentle cleansing of your face on a daily basis.

If the problem is serious, a doctor may be able to provide further help with a prescription drug.

ATHLETE'S FOOT

If you wear socks made of nonbreathing material and if your feet are often wet, the "Foot" may be stomping on your door.

A contagious affliction, athlete's foot can be treated with Micatin, Tinactin, or Zeasorb-AF. Preventive measures include wearing cotton or wool socks, changing them frequently, keeping your shoes dry, wearing thongs in community showers, and drying your feet after showering (maybe even using a blow dryer).

HANGOVERS

Water. Water. Water. More water.

If you are going to drink alcohol at a party, try to alternate between alcoholic and nonalcoholic beverages (e.g., water). Drink a few glasses of water before going to bed as well.

If you wake up feeling dehydrated, you may counter it by drinking—what else?—water.

Time is the only sure cure for a hangover-in-progress, but Alka Seltzer II may make the wait more bearable.

HEADACHES

Because of increased tension, headaches are prevalent in college. To cure them, some recommend tossing down analgesics such as aspirin, acetaminophen, or ibuprofen (e.g., Advil). Take these pharmaceuticals at the onset of a headache, not after the pain has become intolerable.

When aspirin fails, Leslie Friend, a junior at the University of Chicago, suggests having someone massage your neck and scalp. "It works better than you think," Friend said.

For recurring or severe headaches, consult a physician.

SLEEPING PROBLEMS

My roommate never sleeps. I mean, the guy comes in at 5 A.M. every morning and gets up at 9 A.M. Four hours of sleep . . . can you believe it? But, the thing is, he never gets tired. To top it off, he gets mad at me for turning off the lights and going to sleep at 1 A.M. I go to sleep at a normal hour and get yelled at.

—RICK ARNEY, STANFORD UNIVERSITY

Regardless of where you live in college, there will be some students who stay up until 4 A.M. talking about anything from the benefits of liquid soap to the astrophysics of mauve bowling balls. If you cannot stay up this late, don't get trapped by the David Letterman fans. Figure out a way to obtain your required amount of shut-eye. Of course, this varies from person to person. Most can get by with less than they think. Rumor has it Napoleon conquered Europe on just three hours of sleep a day. If you are constantly coming down with infections, however, you are probably one of those people who requires more. You can conquer Europe next year.

Eight to 10 hours of sleep is recommended, especially prior to and during finals week.

SPRAINED ANKLES

Getting through college without spraining your ankle at least once is next to impossible.

If you twist or sprain an ankle, pack it in ice intermittently for 24 to 48 hours—not heat! Bags of frozen peas make good ice packs and can be refrozen and used again.

Immobilize the sprained area with an Ace bandage and elevate it as soon as possible. An anti-inflammatory (e.g., Advil) may help cut down on the pain and swelling. You should see a doctor as soon as possible.

If the swelling or pain seems inordinate, you may have to take more drastic measures. Severe sprains and fractures can be indistinguishable from each other. Immobilize the area, ice it, and seek medical attention pronto.

WHAT ABOUT MEDICAL INSURANCE?

When you broke your arm in sixth grade, you probably were not aware of the cost or the paperwork involved.

Breaking your arm in college is a whole different story. Mom won't be there to hold your hand or to take care of the insurance papers. As Humphrey Bogart said, "You're on your own, kid."

At college, you should consider two medical insurance options:

1. FAMILY MEDICAL INSURANCE

Family medical insurance policies differ in eligibility requirements and coverage. You and your parents should find out if you are still covered under the family's plan. Blue Cross, for example, will provide coverage until a son or daughter turns 23 years old.

While some plans pay for all expenses including prescriptions and hospitalization, other policies cover only major costs such as operations. Before leaving home, understand what your family's plan includes.

2. SCHOOL MEDICAL INSURANCE PLANS

Most schools offer low-cost student medical insurance plans, covering a variety of services. Again, know what you are entitled to under each specific plan.

Basic medical coverage at the University of Washington runs under $800 a year; it is pretty standard around the country.

THE HEALTH SERVICE FEE AT COLLEGE: A NECESSARY EXPENDITURE

In addition to selecting an insurance policy, you may have to pay a health service fee at registration. For roughly $50, you receive medical consultation and psychological counseling. Some schools throw in over-the-counter drugs as well. Although the medical care is notoriously bad at campus health centers, it can come in handy if you sprain your ankle or need a professional diagnosis.

DENTAL HEALTH NEEDS

Have this sharp pain in your mouth? Maybe you need a cavity filled? Thankfully, there is no shortage of dentists.

While many students take care of routine dental work at home, some students like to find a new dentist at college. Ask older students and your dorm advisor who they go to for dental care. Shop around.

 Psst . . . Daily brushing and flossing minimize dental maladies. Remember . . . the extra effort of good oral hygiene more than outweighs the pain and expense of a trip to the dentist's office.

DENTAL PAYMENTS

If you still see your hometown dentist exclusively, the cost will probably be taken care of just as it had been before you went to school. With a new dentist, however, you will have to work out a new payment system. Dental insurance is a good idea.

Below are some examples of typical dental costs in the Seattle area. Rates vary dramatically across the country. Expect to pay more in Chicago than in a small New England town.

Teeth cleaning with routine check-up:	$30–80
Fillings:	$30–80
Crowns:	$300–450
Wisdom Teeth Extractions (all four):	$120–1,200

DENTAL INSURANCE

Dental insurance is independent of health insurance. Like health insurance, however, you may still be covered by your family's dental plan, or you may need to acquire your own.

Know how much of the bill your insurance covers. Will it pay for fillings, crowns, root canals, and teeth cleaning? Find out before taking the "fill."

PSYCHOLOGICAL HEALTH NEEDS

DEPRESSION AND SUICIDE

Although some cannot wait to leave home, others fear the inevitable good-bye. Homesickness affects almost everyone in some way. Many students feel the stress and strain of trying to maintain grades and have a social life at the same time. Others fall into and out of love for the first time. The whole first-year college experience can be quite overwhelming.

The one thing you have to remember is that bouts with depression are *normal*; there is nothing necessarily wrong with you. However, if you are constantly depressed or, worse yet, feeling suicidal, seek help.

Colleges offer counseling to help students, particularly freshmen, through the difficult first year.

Normally, you don't have to pay for this type of counseling. If you seek outside professional help, however, you will assume the cost.

Psst . . . If you see a friend acting strange or particularly depressed, talk to him or her. Ask if he or she is feeling okay. A lot of times, the person is just looking for someone to talk to—someone who cares. If the person does not want to talk and seems suicidal, get professional help. Talk to your resident advisor or contact psychological services in the student health department.

CHAPTER **20**

Nutrition: You Are What You Eat

For the first few weeks of college, I was a madman when it came to the cafeteria. Mom never stocked cola in the fridge at home. Now I could drink it whenever I wanted. Mom never let us eat sugar cereals. Now I could eat Frosted Flakes every morning. Mom never let us skip a main course for two extra desserts. Now I could eat ice cream and jello for the main course.

But, after the first two weeks, I understood why mom never let me have a field day in the kitchen. It wasn't that I was getting fat, although I did put on a few pounds. Rather, I had no energy. I couldn't do my work as fast. I couldn't get to the same balls on the tennis court. I took more naps. Sure enough, I found out that "you are what you eat." Not enough nutritious foods and too much sugar wear you down.

These days I stay away from soda pop and the one or two extra desserts. I feel better, and I work better, too.

—GREG GOTTESMAN, STANFORD UNIVERSITY

NUTRITION TIPS

Upon entering college, you are going to have more freedom than ever before: freedom to stay up all night, freedom to wear your hair anyway you want, and freedom to eat more junk food than you ever imagined!

But there are consequences attached to this new freedom. If you don't eat correctly, you will pay the price in stomach cramps, fatigue, and a wardrobe of clothes one size too small.

As Ben Franklin said, "One should eat to live, not live to eat."

If you sign up for a full or partial meal plan at college, you will have the opportunity to eat healthfully—in your dorm cafeteria or in other food centers on campus. Most cafeterias offer a salad bar, fruit, several entrees, drinks, and a choice of desserts.

Below are six tips for balancing your meals as recommended by the United States Department of Health.

1. Eat a variety of foods from the four food groups: meat, grain, dairy and fruit/vegetables.
2. Avoid too much fat, saturated fat, and cholesterol.
3. Eat foods with adequate starch and fiber.
4. Avoid too much sugar.
5. Avoid too much sodium (salt).
6. If you drink alcoholic beverages, do so in moderation.

AVOIDING THE INFAMOUS "FRESHMAN FIFTEEN"

Face it, Mom didn't let you eat pizza every night, ice cream whenever you wanted, and McDonald's french fries twice a day. She also didn't let you stay up and drink beer with your buddies until dawn. Without knowing it, college students find themselves consuming fatty foods and calorie-filled beverages at double the previous rate. 10 pounds. 15 pounds. 20 pounds. The increments steadily increase while you wolf down another burger or guzzle another beer.

When I went to college, the dorm food was just as bad as it is today. So, after dinner every night, I would devour a pizza, fried chicken, a deli sandwich, or a malted—not to mention a double-scoop Carvel ice-cream cone.

Needless to say, by cleverly eating six meals a day, I gained 15 pounds. It wasn't until an acquaintance referred to me as "that hulky girl" that I realized what I was doing.

—LAURIE MEREDITH WEINMAN, NEW YORK UNIVERSITY

Sherry, a Seattle nutritionist, has provided eight tips to help you keep unwanted weight where it belongs—on other people.

1. If you want to reduce the number of calories in your diet, focus on reducing the amount of fat. By consuming less fat, your calorie intake naturally will be reduced.

2. Increase the amount of fiber in your diet. (Fresh fruits, beans, and legumes are your best bet.)

3. Exercise often.

4. Avoid eating less than four hours before bedtime.

5. Avoid "empty calories," most prevalent in alcohol.

6. Consume six to eight glasses of water daily. Water is useful in metabolizing fat and replacing fluid loss from activity.

7. Don't try to lose more than two pounds per week. Those who try to lose tons of weight all at once are sacrificing muscle and water weight instead of fat.

8. Eat small, frequent meals rather than large, less frequent ones. Large meals, consumed many hours apart, trigger a starvation response, in which the body stores food instead of using it.

Psst . . . Dieting is not always as easy as a trip to the salad bar. In fact, a salad with two helpings of Ranch, Bleu Cheese, or other creamy dressings may have just as many calories as a hot fudge sundae. Be careful!

Most students gain weight their first year of college. I lost.

It wasn't easy. I tried to make dinner a social event rather than an eating event. The hardest things, though, were trying to deal with the late-night munchies and the parties. Alcohol and pizza can put on extra weight like crazy. So, when other people were eating pizza, I chose fruit. When other people were drinking alcohol, I drank water.

It can be done. It just takes hard work and determination.

—JoEllen Tapper, Occidental College

Eating Disorders: Anorexia and Bulimia

Almost every girl I know in college has had an eating disorder at one time or another. Girls with absolutely perfect bodies would come into the dining room and eat everything in sight. Sometimes they would eat really fast and not let anybody see them. You could tell something was wrong.

—Lauren Pass, Grossmont Community College

Thousands of college students, particularly women, suffer from two severe eating disorders: *anorexia nervosa* and *bulimia.*

According to Jacquelin, a registered nurse specializing in eating disorders, the problem usually starts at age 11 or 12 and escalates once in college. Societal pressures and family problems are the two biggest factors leading to the onset of these diseases.

> *I know many women who, when they are stressed about their grades or their boyfriend, automatically blame their problems on their bodies. They turn to crash diets and exercise programs.*
>
> *Don't get me wrong. Concern about your appearance is natural, and exercise and nutrition are extremely important for your health, but too many people ruin their bodies and their lives in a neverending pursuit of thinness.*
>
> —JEANNIE HELTZEL, STANFORD UNIVERSITY

ANOREXIA NERVOSA

Anorexia nervosa, a disease in which victims deliberately starve themselves, can permanently damage the body and, in some cases, lead to death.

Those with this disease feel they are overweight, even if they are not. Symptoms include a severe lack of appetite, low self-esteem, excessive exercise, anxiousness, and a need for isolation.

Lauren Pass, a former anorexic, explains some of the symptoms, "If I ate just once, I wouldn't eat for two weeks after that—at all. I would exercise all the time. Those were the two most obvious signs."

BULIMIA

Those inflicted with *bulimia* binge on large quantities of food and then cleanse their systems through vomiting or laxatives. Symptoms include laxative abuse, dizziness, weakness, and a tendency toward perfectionism.

 Psst . . . You will be doing the suspected bulimic or anorexic a favor by reporting him or her to a dorm advisor or the school health facility.

SECRET DRUGS: CAFFEINE AND ALCOHOL

CAFFEINE: ARE YOU SURE YOU WANT A SECOND CUP?

Many college students pray to the caffeine god. And why not? When a term paper is staring you in the face at 2 A.M., religious symbols provide little solace. Caffeine, on the other hand, can provide pages five through seven.

Found in products such as coffee, cola, chocolate, No Doz, and Vivarin, caffeine, a stimulant, increases your respiration, heart rate, blood pressure, and the secretion of various hormones. Simply, it keeps you awake.

Although not addictive, caffeine is habit-forming. Sudden absence from the drug after long use leads to a withdrawal reaction, the most common symptom being a headache.

The American Heart Association recommends that consumption of caffeine be limited to less than 2 cups of coffee or caffeine-containing beverages per day. Overdoses may cause insomnia, jitteriness, nervousness, and intestinal discomfort.

So, if you are going to use caffeine, do so in moderation.

ALCOHOL: A WHOLE BUNCH OF EMPTY CALORIES?

> *At Colby, we have a game called "Beer Die." You sit at either end of a table and depending on how the die land, someone has to drink. I played it every night for a month straight.*
>
> *The only problem was, after that month, I had built up a serious paunch—a world-class beer belly. I tried to cut back on food but kept drinking. Wouldn't you know it? The paunch stayed. I didn't exactly look like a champion on the beach that summer.*
>
> —CHUCK MARTIN, COLBY COLLEGE

Most people know alcohol kills brain cells and is addictive; it is equally sinister from a nutritional standpoint.

Alcohol fills the body with "empty calories," calories without vitamins, minerals, or protein. These also are referred to as FAT calories. Indeed, the reason many students gain weight in college has nothing to do with increased food intake but, rather, increased alcohol consumption.

So, if you are planning on boozing it up night after night, don't be surprised when the "freshman fifteen" come knocking on your door.

CHAPTER 21

Campus Safety

> As at a lot of schools around the country, campus safety has become a big issue at Duke, particularly for women. The campus is really spread out, so the security people stress walking in groups and keeping to well-lit areas at night. They also have escort services and give all the freshmen whistles in case of an emergency.
>
> I think all that stuff is great. But, let's face it, nothing beats good common sense. The best way to avoid bad situations is to not get into them in the first place. I always try to be aware of where I am and who I am with. I don't walk in "questionable" areas alone. I don't put myself in situations where bad things are likely to happen.
>
> —HEIDI WIEDEMANN, DUKE UNIVERSITY

BE AWARE AND ALERT!

Here are 10 safety tips for college campuses. The first five concern protecting yourself outdoors and the next five inside your dormitory or Greek house.

Remember that these tips are not intended to make you paranoid. Just the opposite, in fact. They should make you feel like you have some control over your own safety, which you do, of course.

If you forget some of these tips, don't worry. Just remember the general idea that they all uphold: Use good common sense—which is the last and grand finale tip. This means always being alert and being aware of your surroundings.

1. STICK WITH GROUPS, ESPECIALLY AT NIGHT

> *A lot of the women at Harvard ask us to walk them to the science center at night. It's a pretty long walk, but none of the guys mind. The women are never embarrassed to ask us, and we always do it. We just see it as a small way we can make our classmates feel a little more safe.*
>
> —ROBERT LLOYD, HARVARD UNIVERSITY

Whether you're coming back from the library or returning home after a party, avoid walking alone. Sometimes it's easy to forget the simple truth: there is safety in numbers.

Don't feel embarrassed about asking a friend to walk you back to your room, preferably a male if you are a female. He or she probably will be flattered anyway.

And don't be afraid to use the campus escort services or safe rides. Most of the time the escorts are just waiting to be called upon. Use them; that's what they're there for.

2. DON'T JOG ALONE, ESPECIALLY AT NIGHT

This tip seems pretty similar to the last one. Want to know why? Because it is ... seriously, it cannot be repeated enough. Even students who are careful to walk in groups at night seem to forget this precaution when going out for a midnight or early-morning jog. Especially if you are a female, try to bring a companion.

3. WALK BRISKLY AND WITH PURPOSE

> *My friends often make fun of me because I walk so fast. And sometimes they'll be following me for blocks before we realize that we have no idea where we're headed. This is because I never dawdle or walk as if I don't know exactly where I'm going. Granted, there are times when whizzing past everyone prevents me from smelling the roses. But, as my New York background has taught me, it's always better to be safe than sorry.*
>
> —NOELEEN WALDER, STANFORD UNIVERSITY

It is always a good idea to look like you know where you're going, especially when walking alone. This means moving quickly and with some sort of purpose. Stopping a lot and talking to strangers often leads to trouble. Of course, this doesn't mean you should be suspicious of everyone who asks you a question. But use your intuition when strangers approach.

Also, don't be afraid to be rude. Your safety is much more important than the impression you give a stranger.

4. STAY IN WELL-LIT, POPULATED AREAS

In general, it is a good idea to avoid dark areas. Don't take shortcuts unless you know they are well-traveled and well-lit. Campus police departments often prepare maps of suggested travel routes. If you have any doubts about which are the safest routes, use the maps.

5. DON'T FLASH VALUABLES

Don't wear your fancy jewelry around the campus everyday. Flashy items attract attention and make you an easy target.

You'll have plenty of opportunities to show off your best duds and jewelry at semi-formals and so forth. In the meantime, leave the diamonds and the gold hidden in your room.

Also, remember to keep your purse zipped. It is easy to lose valuables when you set down a floppy handbag, and you don't want people eyeing your wallet.

 Psst . . . When you are moving through large crowds from class to class, it is better to keep your purse over your shoulder rather than clutched in your hand. Thieves will have a harder time grabbing something over your shoulder as opposed to snatching a bag out of your hand.

6. KEEP A LIST OF EMERGENCY NUMBERS HANDY

You never know when you are going to have to call for help. And given the state of most college rooms, it is doubtful you will be able to find the telephone book at a moment's notice. So, keep a list of important numbers near the phone. You can even tape the list to the phone itself.

If you are in trouble and cannot figure out who to call, dial 911 . . . that's usually your best bet.

7. LOCK YOUR DOORS

College campuses are notorious for theft. This doesn't mean you have to be suspicious of your next-door neighbor. Thieves from the local area know that college students tend to be apathetic about locking their doors, and they take advantage of it. So, take your keys with you and lock your door—always!

When I first got to school, I used to leave the door unlocked when I went to the shower. But about four weeks into the quarter, that policy changed in a hurry.

It was about 4 P.M., and I had just taken a shower after a rough basketball game. As I walked back into my room with only a towel covering me, I nearly bumped into a rather large man. Nope, it wasn't my roommate. I wish. The stranger was about 6-feet-4 and, let me tell you, he obviously had been to the gym a few times.

In the meantime, he seemed to be depositing several of the items on my roommate's desk into his pockets. His back was turned, and I politely asked him, terrified of course, "Excuse me, but what do you think you're doing in my room?"

I obviously surprised him. He spun around and said, "Um, can you tell me where the basketball arena is?"

"Well, it's certainly not in here," I said. "It's about five miles down the road."

He looked at me and ran out the door.

Needless to say, from that time on, my roommate and I locked our door whenever we were out of the room—even if we were just going to the shower.

—ALEX BERZINS, STANFORD UNIVERSITY

8. DON'T LET STRANGERS INTO THE DORMITORY

One of the best ways to protect yourself and your classmates at college is to prevent problems before they hatch. Not letting strangers into your dorm is the simplest and most effective way to do just that.

The doors to most college dormitories are locked. So, when a stranger wants to get in, don't be afraid to ask him or her the reason for the visit. If the stranger is associated with the campus, he or she will be more than happy to state his or her intent.

Also, try not to prop the doors open at night. Sure, waiting for the pizza delivery man by the door can be a drag, especially at 1 A.M. But, if you leave the door open, you are just begging for trouble.

9. BE CAREFUL IN THE ELEVATORS

Big dormitories at big schools usually have elevators, and these can be a major source of problems.

Avoid riding up or down in the elevator with strangers, especially if you are a woman. If someone makes you feel uneasy while riding, get off at the next floor. Your safety is definitely worth the extra wait.

In addition, if the door opens and you don't like the contents, act as if you forgot something, walk away, and take the next elevator.

10. STAY CALM AND USE COMMON SENSE

These 10 tips may be helpful, but they certainly cannot take the place of simple common sense. College life will present you with many new situations. You will be living in your own room. You will be able to set your own hours. You will be able to attend parties or other social gatherings almost every night. Obviously you are not going to lock yourself up in a room. But there are dangers of which you should be aware.

The best advice, once again, is to use good common sense. Stay calm. Be aware of the situation you are in at all times.

And don't be afraid to leave a party if it is getting out of hand or to "embarrass" someone if you feel uncomfortable.

DATE RAPE: THE REALITY ON COLLEGE CAMPUSES

> *Officials at the University of Southern California and the Los Angeles Police Department are investigating a student's report that she was raped in a fraternity house while on a date last September and subjected to a party of mostly undressed [fraternity] members.*
>
> *The student said the rape took place . . . last September. But police said she did not file a formal complaint until April.*
>
> —*The New York Times*, June 24, 1990

Date rape has become one of the biggest issues facing American colleges today. Date rape is defined as forced, manipulated, or coerced sexual acts by a friend or acquaintance occurring in a date-like situation. Below are three scary truths about date rape on college campuses today.

FACT 1:

> *In a recent survey of over 6,000 students from over 32 colleges across the country, one out of every six female students reported being a victim of rape or attempted rape during the preceding year.*
>
> —A. ADAMS, *Sexual Assault On Campus*, 1988

FACT 2:

Ninety-four percent of all rapes are committed by an acquaintance.

—D. RUSSELL, *Rape in Marriage*, 1982

FACT 3:

In a Kent State University study, one in 12 men admitted to having fulfilled the prevailing definition of rape or attempted rape, yet none of these men identified themselves as rapists.

—M. KOSS, *Ms.* Magazine Campus Project on Sexual Assault, 1988

TIPS TO HELP YOU AVOID DATE RAPE

BE AWARE OF THE EFFECT OF ALCOHOL AND DRUGS

Drinking, especially beyond your "limit," interferes with clear thinking and effective communication. "Against Her Will," a cable television program on Lifetime, asserted that 75 percent of the men and 55 percent of the women are intoxicated during date rape.

Learn your limit—both men and women. Don't get so drunk that you do things you will regret the next day.

 Psst ... Having sexual intercourse with someone who is drunk or, more specifically, a person who is incapable of resisting, is considered rape in a court of law.

COMMUNICATE YOUR LIMITS CLEARLY

If someone starts to offend you or make you feel uncomfortable, tell this person firmly and immediately that he or she is doing something you don't like. Say no when you mean no. Say it loudly and clearly.

PAY ATTENTION TO WHAT IS HAPPENING AROUND YOU

Watch for nonverbal clues (e.g., if someone is touching you more than you are comfortable with). Try not to put yourself in vulnerable situations.

If you feel uncomfortable, the best thing to do is to leave. A lot of times a person will not want to offend the other party by making an early exit. Baloney! Your personal safety should come first.

DON'T BLAME YOURSELF

If you are raped, a common reaction is to blame yourself. Don't do it! Nobody asks to be raped!

Seek emotional support and see a doctor immediately for treatment of injuries or a rape exam.

THINK ABOUT REPORTING THE INCIDENT

Ultimately, reporting a rape is your decision. But the police encourage it for several reasons. First, an immediate report will allow valuable evidence to be collected. This increases the chance of apprehension and a successful prosecution.

Second, you will be providing official documentation necessary for criminal prosecution or civil redress if you later choose to pursue this course of action.

Finally, many rapists are repeat offenders. You will be providing information on a person who could be responsible for other assaults, thereby protecting yourself as well as others.

CHAPTER 22

Banking at College

> Before I went to college, I didn't realize how many things I spent money on . . . food, gas, pencils, paper, books, clothes, and that's just for starters.
>
> If you think you can make it at college with just a few hundred dollars of spending money, you're kidding yourself. Going to a formal can run well over a hundred bucks, and that's not including the corsage.
>
> If you're going to college, you're definitely going to need some spending money. And you're definitely going to need a bank to store it in.
>
> —JUSTIN KENNEDY, WESLEYAN UNIVERSITY

LOOK OUT FOR HIDDEN EXPENSES!

Hidden expenses often take college students by surprise. Most expect just the tuition bill and fees for room and board, but the other expenditures like midnight pizzas and textbooks add up to well over a few Andrew Jacksons. In other words, you cannot just stuff a few $20 bills in your wallet before you leave home and expect to survive. You need a bank.

CHOOSING A BANK

When choosing a bank, keep two things in mind:

1. Find a bank that has ATMs (automatic teller machines) within walking distance of your room.

2. Consider all possible hidden costs of the bank in question.

> *When choosing a bank, the important thing is to know what you want. What I needed was the basic services for the cheapest possible price. Every single bank has fees, whether they tell you about them or not.*
>
> —Ann Wilensky, Columbia University

Although most banks offer similar services, fees fluctuate. If you are not careful, you could end up paying $150 a year in service fees, more than twice what is necessary.

Taking Money to College

If you are transferring money from a savings account at your hometown bank to one at school, request a cashier's check for the amount you want to take. The cost for a cashier's check will be minimal, if anything at all.

Consider leaving your hometown account open, because you probably will want to use it when you come home for holidays and summer vacation.

When opening a new account at school, a cashier's check may take a few days to clear, especially if you go to school out-of-state. You should consider purchasing a couple hundred dollars in travelers checks to buy essentials. Travelers checks cost approximately $1.50 per $100. If your parents belong to a credit union or have a sizable bank account, they may be eligible for free travelers checks. American Automobile Association (AAA) members can also receive free travelers checks from AAA offices.

FORGET WESTERN UNION!

Don't send your money to college by wire transfer. A bank charges you to send the money out, and then the receiving bank charges you again. The result is a loss of $15-$20. Western Union is even worse, charging you between $20-$41. The only advantage to this method is that it's speedy.

BANKING AT AN IN-STATE SCHOOL

Those who have chosen a local university should have no trouble selecting a bank.

If an ATM of your hometown bank is located near the university, stick with it. You will be able to do almost all necessary transactions without having to transfer your account.

SELECTING THE BEST ACCOUNT FOR YOUR NEEDS

If you are changing banks and need to open a new account, decide which banks are most popular among the students and pay them a visit.

When you enter a potential bank, walk up to an official behind a desk—not a teller—and inform him or her that you are thinking of opening an account. The banker may load you with scads of pamphlets. Be careful! Obtain literature only on those services that concern you: savings, checking, ATMs, and credit cards.

Make sure to ask if the bank offers a special student package. These plans are definitely worth looking into as they usually offer free or reduced service charges on ATMs as well as other incentives.

Also inquire about ATM charges on your bank's machine *and* other banks' machines. You will be using the ATM a lot. Choose an account with minimal or no ATM charges.

SAVINGS, CHECKING, AND MONEY MARKET ACCOUNTS

Before deciding which account or combination of accounts you need, understand the three different types of accounts: checking, savings and money market.

CHECKING ACCOUNTS

Because you will have some big bills to pay at college, you should get a checking account. Banks generally have three types of checking accounts: normal, limited, and interest-bearing.

The *normal option* requires a minimum balance of $300–$500. If you stay above this balance, the bank charges no monthly fee. Falling below results in a penalty charge. The disadvantage of this option is that you earn no interest.

The *limited-option* checking account enforces no minimum balance and lets you write up to 10 checks a month—more than enough for a college student. This account often costs about $1.75 a month. With the limited option, you can take the minimum balance you had in the normal option (around $300) and put it into savings. This will earn roughly $20 dollars in interest throughout the year. Of course, with the limited option account, you pay about $20 a year in monthly checking fees. Before making a decision, realize that many banks offer special limited accounts to students in which no fee is charged for checks or for monthly use. This could be your best bet.

For those with a very nice nest egg, an *interest-bearing* checking account allows you to earn interest while keeping your money available for checking. In most cases, you can earn interest as long as your average monthly balance does not dip below $1,000–2,500 at any time. The charge when letting your account slip below the required minimum is rather steep. If you have the available funds and remain wary, an interest-bearing checking account may be . . . well, wasn't it Siskel and Ebert who said . . . "two thumbs up"?

SAVINGS ACCOUNTS

Usually $100–$300 will open a savings account. Regardless of the bank you choose, these accounts pay around five percent interest, more than an average checking account. There should be no charge for depositing or withdrawing money.

On the negative side, you cannot write checks with a savings account. Furthermore, if your account drops below the minimum assigned by the bank (e.g., $100), you will be charged a slight fee.

While some banks compound interest annually, others quarterly, and others daily, computer analysis shows it makes only a miniscule difference in earnings at year's end.

Because interest rates and interest earnings rarely vary, the three most important criteria for judging a savings account should be:

1. What is the minimum balance?
2. How much do I get charged if I dip beneath the minimum balance?
3. Is there any fee for using the ATM?

Many students opt for a savings account along with a checking account. They keep most of their money in their savings account, which earns higher interest, and transfer funds when their checking account dwindles.

MONEY MARKET ACCOUNTS

The money market account has several advantages:

1. It offers you a higher rate of interest than the normal checking account as long as you maintain a minimum balance.

2. It does not require a monthly service fee above the minimum balance.

The disadvantage is that often you are allowed only three checks per month, leaving just one for tuition, one for housing, and the last for the phone bill. If you do write an extra check or if your account slips below the minimum balance, the bank charges you a stiff fee. Also, most banks do not let you earn interest when you go below the minimum balance.

DEPOSITING MONEY: USE THE ATM!

Each time you receive money, whether it be a paycheck or that $20 bill Grandpa handed you beneath the dinner table, you should deposit it immediately into your bank account. By depositing your money as quickly as possible, you avoid losing it and start earning interest, depending on your account.

The easiest and fastest way to deposit funds is to use the ATM. Don't fear ATMs! They are extremely accurate and will never swallow up your money for no reason.

Go to the ATM machine, usually open 24 hours a day, and insert your card. The machine then will ask you for your access code.

 Psst . . . Never tell anyone about this code, not even your roommate. You can always find a better way to get some money. Don't let anybody use your card!

Once you enter your code, the machine will ask you what kind of transaction you want. In this case, you press "deposit." You will then be asked to input the amount. If you input the wrong number, simply press "correction" and start over.

After you have typed in the amount, the machine will tell you to insert the envelope containing your check into a special compartment. Make sure you endorse the back of the check with your signature, along with the words "for deposit only" and your account number. With regard to your account number, you may have different ones for your various accounts: checking, savings, and/or money market. Make sure you write down the correct one. Once that is done, the machine will issue you a receipt and you're on your way. Not so fast! Don't forget to take your card out of the machine and don't forget to record the transaction in your checkbook—whether it be a deposit or a withdrawal.

COMMON PROBLEMS AT THE ATMS

ATMs allow you to bank without ever actually entering one— a bank, that is. But, despite making banking a lot easier, ATMs bring some new problems to the world of finance.

DON'T LOSE YOUR CARD

If you lose your ATM card, call the bank as soon as possible. Most banks have 24-hour numbers, which you should have on file both in your wallet and in your dorm room.

DON'T GO TO THE ATM ALONE AT NIGHT

Try to go to the ATMs during the day, especially if your bank is in the city. If you do have to use one at night, go with a friend.

DON'T ABUSE YOUR ATM PRIVILEGES

ATMs make it extremely easy to withdraw money. After pushing the "withdraw" button too many times, you may begin to think your ATM card is a product of the devil. But, if you keep good records and remember to record your withdrawals and deposits, you shouldn't have any problems.

KEEPING TRACK OF YOUR CHECKING ACCOUNT

Many college students don't see the purpose behind recording checks and deposits. Doesn't the bank do it anyway? Hold the phone!

Not only do good records bar you from dipping below the minimum balance and being charged a fee, they also prevent you from overdrafting your account (having a negative balance).

Besides, banks make errors! At the end of a month, the bank will send a statement with all your banking transactions. This will include an outline of the amount withdrawn, the amount deposited, and the amount deducted in fees and charges. The balance you have at the bottom of your checkbook should match exactly the balance that the bank sends you, excluding any deposits and/or checks that have not cleared (see the formula that follows). If the two do not match and you have rechecked your figures carefully, call the bank.

THE FORMULA

Your Balance = Bank's Balance − Uncleared Checks + Uncleared Deposits

 Psst . . . One of the best ways to keep adequate records is to order duplicate checks. This type of check has a carbon copy behind each original check. Everything you write on the original is reprinted on the carbon copy. Thus, if you

forget to enter an amount, you can always go back and check the stack of duplicates.

YOU ARE IN DEMAND!

Selecting the "right" bank and the "right" combination of accounts can fluster even the most organized student. With so many banks to choose from and so many options to sift through, students often forget who is in the driver's seat.

You are!

Realizing that today's college graduates will be tomorrow's achievers, banks are vying for your business. They want to establish a financial relationship with you, hoping it will continue in the future.

If you remember who is in control, who the desired customer is, and whose business the banks want, selecting a bank becomes much less intimidating.

CREDIT CARDS

If your friends try to impress you by whipping out a credit card to pay for something, you can laugh at them. Almost anyone over 18 can get a credit card, especially college students. Banks that offer credit cards are dying for new, young business.

In the simplest of terms, credit cards allow you to pay for an item a month after the actual purchase. If you are unable to pay after the month, however, you will be assessed interest. For example, VISA, MasterCard, gas companies and department store credit cards start financing the amount you cannot pay immediately after your billing period has concluded; this means they will charge you an exorbitant rate of interest—almost 20 percent annually—on the money you cannot pay.

American Express is even more strict. It subjects you to heavy penalties if you cannot pay the entire amount after your billing period.

Be careful! Remember the little boy who filled his plate so full of food because his eyes were bigger than his stomach. Don't charge more than you can afford.

If you are continually late with payments or you cannot pay at all, these credit card companies may take the worst revenge of all: destroying your credit rating. This rating is extremely important later in life when you want to take out a loan for a car or a home.

Your credit rating is so important that many students get a credit card just to establish a good rating. If you are consistent with your payments, your rating will go up.

> *I have an American Express Card but never use it. It helps for identification purposes or for an emergency where I might need some quick cash in the middle of nowhere. It also helps build my credit rating for the future.*
>
> —HUNTER GOODMAN,
> UNIVERSITY OF SOUTHERN CALIFORNIA

The annual membership fees vary with each card as well. American Express usually has a higher yearly fee than VISA or MasterCard. If you are interested in a credit card, you first should consider special student deals, offered by most of the major banks.

In sum, when used wisely, credit cards are convenient and an excellent way to pay for certain items. But don't ask for trouble by charging more than you can afford.

LAST BUT NOT LEAST: A WORD ON BUDGETING

> *It is difficult to learn the meaning of fiscal responsibility, especially when you've got a new VISA and there's a great-looking sweater in the shop window. It's even harder when the sweater is on sale.*
>
> *My mom told me not to go over $200 on my card. I had finals to take and, as my apartment was off-campus, I rented a car for finals week, hoping to use my free time for study. During the month, I had charged a few sweaters and a pair of jeans but no item totalling more than $40. Just things I really needed.*
>
> *I was shocked when I got my VISA bill. $600! No joke. I guess I did not realize how much I was spending with the rental car and all. Believe me, it's incredibly easy to run up a VISA bill without even knowing it.*
>
> *My first lesson in banking: Keep good records, not only in your checkbook but also on your credit card. Lesson number two: Don't buy more than you can afford.*
>
> —LAUREN PASS, GROSSMONT COMMUNITY COLLEGE

Budgeting goes hand-in-hand with banking. You and your parents should *write out* a spending plan. Be realistic and remember to include entertainment costs, housing, books, food, clothing, laundry, and lab fees.

Once at school, try to record daily expenditures in a budget book—for the first few weeks, anyway. When you realize how much you are spending on midnight pizzas and the local fast-food restaurant, you may think twice. A listing, in black and white, of how the money is evaporating, will force you to be fiscally aware and also prevent future catastrophes.

CHAPTER 23

Community Colleges

I was able to take community college classes during my senior year in high school. It was great. I felt so grown up. My experience was very positive. I took college-level classes and one college-prep class in English. I decided to enroll after high school. I wasn't sure what I wanted to major in and besides, my grandmother was paying my tuition. I am taking all college transfer classes now and have my plans made to transfer after two years. I also got a great part-time job through an internship, and since my college is near downtown, I can work after classes. I've met so many different people in my classes. I realize that I am young and have lots of learning to do. I am glad the community college was here for me.

—RACHEL TITUS, SEATTLE CENTRAL COMMUNITY COLLEGE

Before my divorce was final, I knew I wanted to get back to the degree I had never finished. I found a community college in my area that had a strong college transfer program. There I was, the age of most of my fellow students mothers, yet we all got along, worked to form study groups, and learned from each other. I graduated with honors on the dean's list, went on to get my B.A., and am now enrolled in a master's program to be a counselor. The community college gave me a second start.

—CORRIE GOLUB, SHORELINE COMMUNITY COLLEGE

WHY GO TO COMMUNITY COLLEGE?

If you're starting your foray into higher education at a community college, you're in good company. Fifty percent of undergraduates in this country are in community colleges, just like you.

When you tell mom and dad, or aunts and uncles, that you are going to a community college, they often are not sure what you mean. If they have not been watching the college scene in the past 20 years, they may be thinking about some junior college they heard of a long time ago that seemed to be for kids who had problems.

That's not you at all. You are a participant in one of the greatest experiments and adventures in higher education in this century. You are a part of a student body that spans all ages, races, languages, and levels of ability. You are enrolled in higher education that offers a tremendous amount of opportunity with smaller class sizes and a smaller price tag.

"Community" colleges do just that: they serve their communities. This means that you are probably living near home and attending a community college that is mostly a commuter school and does not house students in dorms, fraternities, or sororities.

These are the strengths of your community college:

1. You can live at home or on your own.

2. You can attend full time or part time, depending upon your situation. A large percentage of community college students work full or part time.

3. Your college is probably small enough that you can get involved in any kind of student activities that you wish.

How To Make the Best of Your Time

If you haven't already taken a look at the breadth of offerings at your college, this might be a good time to do it. Most community colleges have at least three kind of programs that you can choose from:

1. COLLEGE PREPARATORY OR PRE-COLLEGE PROGRAMS

Not all of the students who enter community college are writing, reading, or doing math at a college level. So, most community colleges test incoming students in these areas. If you need brush-up or review, you can get it at your community college.

Advice: If you need college-prep reading, English composition, or math, take those pre-college classes early on—don't let them hold up your plans. For example, many students wait until they're ready to transfer before taking pre-college math. The math class ends up being an unnecessary roadblock to transferring. By taking the college-prep courses early on, you also enable yourself to succeed in other classes. For instance, college-prep composition will help you to write better research papers and make you feel more comfortable during the writing sections of exams.

> *I started community college several times. But the time I was successful, I started it by taking the math and English that I needed to get up to college level. I moved quickly through the college-prep program and began to take college level courses. I finished my courses, transferred to the state university, and found that all of the good teaching I had had really helped me. I got my degree in Business Administration using the skills I had picked up studying with groups and being in small classes with instructor attention.*
>
> —Jabari Grant, University of Washington

2. VOCATIONAL PROGRAMS

Most community colleges offer two-year vocational programs that lead directly into the job market. Many colleges are known for certain types of these programs. For example, some community colleges specialize in the biomedical field, computer technology, culinary arts, drafting, automotive, and so on. Check out the vocational programs at your community college. See if one of the fields interests you, especially if you are undecided about what kind of education you want and what you will do with it.

3. COLLEGE TRANSFER PROGRAMS

A large number of students are enrolled in community colleges to get the first two years of their college career in a smaller, less stressful environment that is more economical. If you fall into this category, here are some quick tips:

- See a college transfer counselor early on
- Plan out your classes for your freshman and sopho-more years to ensure you meet all the requirements
- Make sure you are enrolling in *transferable* classes
- Check out the transfer agreements between your college and universities in the area
- Speak with representatives from four-year colleges when they visit your campus
- If four-year college representatives do not visit, get in touch with the university where you want to transfer and find out about any unusual requirements

Community colleges offer several degrees. Even if you are planning to transfer to a four-year college for your Bachelor of Arts (B.A.) degree, you still may want to consider an Associate of Arts (A.A.) degree. This A.A. degree is awarded when you accomplish what would be your freshman and sophomore years. It is great for putting on a resume or job application. Check out the requirements for an A.A. on your campus and then decide if you want to try to meet those requirements. Some students just want to transfer to start working toward their B.A. and skip the A.A.

> *I first started community college out of high school because it was the most economical choice for me. I did well in college transfer classes, but did not have enough money to support myself. I left college and enrolled in a beauty school program. When I graduated, I got a job as a manicurist and returned to community college using my skills to support myself. I graduated with my A.A. and went on to major in economics and get my B.A. I supported myself the whole time. I even met my husband at the community college, and we transferred together. I now own my own business.*
>
> —JANNETTE HOFMANN, SEATTLE UNIVERSITY

WHAT SHOULD YOU TAKE ADVANTAGE OF WHILE YOU ARE AT COMMUNITY COLLEGE?

1. SAVE MONEY FOR A RAINY DAY.

You are spending far less on a comparable education. Be aware of it! Save now, so you will have a cushion when you need it, perhaps while pursuing a more expensive education.

2. TAKE ADVANTAGE OF SMALLER CLASSES AND SMALLER STUDENT-TEACHER RATIOS.

Community colleges are known as teaching, not research, institutions. The instructors are hired to teach, not bury themselves in the library. You will have small classes in the 25-35 student range. These classes are taught by instructors who want to teach you—get to know them. Take classes from the instructors you like and avoid the ones you don't.

3. MEET OTHER STUDENTS.

Community colleges have diverse student bodies. Make an effort to meet the students in your classes. Form study groups. Don't be afraid of the woman who is your mother's age. (She may be the one getting the A's!) Learn about other cultures. Listen to the experiences of people who have been out there for longer than you have.

4. GET INVOLVED IN ACTIVITIES.

A community college is small enough for you to get involved in student leadership or other activities. In the process, you will get to know other students and have a few items to fill in those blank spots on your resume or job applications.

With two young children, I never thought I would be able to return to college. I went to a vocational training program, but I was disappointed in the training. A friend told me about Seattle Central Community College. I applied for financial aid and was accepted. I started school with no idea how I would do it, but by using all the resources available to me, I really did well. I took a few college-prep classes to review and I found that when I got into my college-level classes, I was the student getting As and Bs. I joined the national honor society with a chapter on my campus and, before I knew it, I was president. So here was me—single mother, honor society president, and, when I graduated with my A.A., I was chosen graduation speaker and given a scholarship. I don't know where I would have been without this opportunity.

—GEORGETTE BROOKS, UNIVERSITY OF WASHINGTON

CHAPTER 24

Working at School

A guy who lived in my dorm desperately wanted to find a job. But minimum wage, for him, was untenable. More simply, he wanted a job that would pay him adequately for his services.

After several weeks of frantic job-searching, nothing surfaced. Then, strolling merrily into my room one afternoon, he told me he'd found his pot of gold, a job that "suited" him perfectly.

He had found employment in the arts—specifically, in the field of nude photography. And, let me just say, he wasn't the one taking the pictures.

While the job paid well, some of my more modest friends were paid equally well working graveyard shifts for a delivery service. Sure enough, if you're willing to endure unusual working conditions, healthy salaries are available.

—STEVE OJEMANN, UNIVERSITY OF WASHINGTON

QUESTIONS TO ASK BEFORE THE JOB SEARCH

Before beginning a search for employment at college, ask yourself these five key questions:

1. WHY SHOULD YOU GET A JOB?

For some, the answer boils down to economics or, more specifically, the financing of a college education. For others, reasons for getting a job include work experience, references, and, of course, resume padding. Regardless of the specific reason, knowledge of why you are getting a job may help you answer the next question.

2. WHAT TYPE OF JOB SHOULD YOU GET?

Basically, three types of jobs exist: volunteer, research (which often yields college credit), and paid work.

The first category, volunteer work, bequeaths no money. But it often serves purposes more admirable than other types of employment. Having a volunteer job can lead to excellent future paying jobs, garner character recommendations, and look impressive on a resume.

The second type, in which college credit supersedes payment, takes some time to find but offers flexibility and, for the most part, no homework. A college advisor or job-placement service will ease the burden of a search for this type of job, often referred to as an assistantship, clerkship, or research preceptorship.

The final category of work includes all the miscellaneous jobs in which one is compensated for his or her services. Lack of experience may limit the job choices in this category to working in a fast-food restaurant or an equivalent. But don't fret! As you get older and more experienced, your opportunities will expand.

A subdivision under the "paying job" category called "work-study" provides financially needy students with jobs paying higher-than-normal wages. These jobs, which require those interested to prove financial need, serve as pseudo-scholarships enabling some students to afford college. Generally, work-study jobs have the student working in a campus cafeteria or the office of a faculty member.

3. HOW MUCH TIME WILL THE JOB TAKE?

Don't fool yourself. Any serious working schedule is going to take a huge chunk of time out of your day and force you to make some big sacrifices.

But it can be done. I worked three jobs during college—at a pizza parlor, a men's clothing store, and in an athletic supply. In my free time, I even set up my own business. I had T-shirts made up and hired a crew to sell them for a profit. I paid for school that way.

I certainly wouldn't recommend this type of working schedule for everyone, though, especially if it starts negatively impacting on your grades. See how much time you can afford to work and then go from there.

For me, it was a matter of making every second of every day count. I learned to manage my time so effectively that I could work over 30 hours a week, maintain decent grades, and even play varsity rugby. It mostly depends on the types of jobs you have and the type of person you are.

—SEAN M. MCTAGGART, UNIVERSITY OF PITTSBURGH

Before committing to any set number of hours, settle into a college schedule and determine the amount of study and free time available. Most employers sympathize with students and agree to a flexible work schedule with time off for mid-terms and finals.

The amount of time you have for work should depend on the number and difficulty of classes. Assuming a fairly standard college load of three or four classes, most working students agree that 10 to 20 hours a week is more than an ample time commitment for work.

A potential danger in working at school is getting involved in a job that requires time off-the-job or, more explicitly, job-related homework. Be wary of jobs that claim to demand only a fixed amount of time each week and then expect extra at-home work. Realize that certain jobs have unusual demands. University of Washington junior John Schreuder warns, "A harmless flower-delivery job, which usually takes three hours a day, can become a nightmare on Mother's Day when deliveries increase tenfold."

4. SHOULD YOU GET AN ON-CAMPUS OR OFF-CAMPUS JOB?

There are three major factors you need to take into account before answering this question: desirability, wages, and transportation. Basically, you want to obtain the most desirable job that is easy to get to with the highest wages.

At large universities, on-campus jobs of this sort may be plentiful. At smaller private schools, however, finding a desirable on-campus job may be more difficult. But, before going off-campus, make sure to consider transportation. You don't want to be walking eight miles to work at 5 A.M. because no other means of transportation are available.

5. WHAT ARE SOME JOBS YOU CAN GET?

Now that you have some questions to hash over, you undoubtedly are interested in what specific jobs are available to college students. While off-campus jobs vary depending upon the setting of the campus, on-campus jobs remain fairly similar throughout the country.

Attractive benefits of these university-sponsored jobs include reasonable pay and flexible hours. Several common university-sponsored jobs include:

Food service jobs: Duties include serving meals, preparing food, and performing custodial work.

University libraries: Libraries always need people to help with checking out and reshelving books.

Tutoring positions: Many larger schools have a student tutoring service sponsored by the university.

Recreational sports programs: This usually involves managing and organizing intramural sports activities.

Ticket offices: Most colleges have at least one or two ticket outlets for sporting and special events such as plays and art exhibitions.

Copy centers: Universities will often use students to staff copy centers because barely any experience is needed to fulfill the post.

Parking division: This includes enforcing parking rules on campus and running visitor parking facilities.

Residence halls: Employment in a residence hall may range from clerical to custodial work. Resident Advisors (RAs) also are needed.

Clerical work: Many departments need students who have office skills such as typing.

Ground maintenance: In this line of work, duties may vary from gardening to custodial or even window-washing.

 Psst . . . If you are lucky, you can find work doing something you ordinarily would do for free. For example, many college newspapers and yearbooks offer salaried positions for writers and editors. Many would-be journalists can make a pretty penny doing something they love.

In addition, the advertising departments of campus publications are always looking for advertising representatives. These jobs usually pay well, offering you a percentage of your sales.

Trying the Entrepreneurial Route

> *Our tennis team needed money for equip-*
> *ment, so I decided to put my entrepreneurial*
> *talents to the test. I obtained the rights from*
> *both the Lowenbrau beer corporation and UPS*
> *to use their logos. Then I bought 200 mugs*
> *and put the Lowenbrau and UPS insignias on*
> *all 200. The team sold the mugs at the fall*
> *season football games, and I made a nice*
> *profit for the team.*
>
> —KEITH VERNON, UNIVERSITY OF PUGET SOUND

If the typical jobs don't appeal to you, you can try the entrepreneurial route. College students have made more than
pocket change selling T-shirts, mugs, Greek swimsuit calen-
dars, videos of the campus, and so on.

An entrepreneur always thinks in terms of supply and
demand, a true capitalist to the end. If something is needed
at your school, the successful entrepreneur provides it—at a
price, of course!

Keep in mind that entrepreneurial schemes are risky. If you
really need the money for tuition or books, some of the other
jobs are more practical.

Where Do You Look and Who Do You Ask?

In many cases, the answer to where to look for a job should
be apparent. For example, if a volunteer job in the health
sciences is the goal, simply contact a local hospital. On the
other hand, if no specific job has distinguished itself, sev-

eral resources might help. Below is a list of three resources at your disposal.

1. FRIENDS AND RELATIVES

The best source of job information comes from word-of-mouth communication; someone tells you about a job opening, and you pursue it.

Friends and family members can be invaluable when it comes to this kind of information. Once they know you are searching for a job, they may notice ads in the newspaper or signs in windows. More often, a friend or relative may know someone who has a job opening and may be able to "pull a few strings" for you. You have heard the expression: It doesn't matter what you know but who you know. Well, the expression didn't get famous for nothing!

2. UNIVERSITY RESOURCES

Most universities have a career placement office through which you can find some invaluable information. Counselors in these offices can help you locate a job and give you some advice on applying for one as well.

In addition, many schools have computer systems that contain listings of job openings classified and referenced by job type, location, pay, applicant's experience and various other criteria. At many large schools, the computer list of jobs is updated daily and contains valuable information such as the employer's telephone number and time commitment desired.

3. OTHER PLACES TO LOOK

In most cases, employers will post signs, take out ads in a newspaper, or in some way make "public" their desire for employees. If you have your heart set on working for a specific company, which is not advertising, calling and asking for a job never hurts; the employer might be impressed that you took the initiative.

APPLYING FOR THE JOB

For most university-sponsored jobs such as food service, you will not need to apply. You may just call up an office and be told to meet at the job site in the morning.

But for more prestigious university jobs and summer employment, the application process is crucial.

Still, the most helpful piece of advice available is: "Don't worry!" Everyone has faced rejection—more than once—and lived to tell about it. Don't let your lack of experience invoke anguish. As University of Washington sophomore Katie MacDonald said, "If they are offering a job to students, usually they don't expect a rocket scientist. If they get someone who is honest and reliable, they're happy."

The following sections provide tips on job applications, interviews, and resumes. Pay special attention to the sample resume and cover letter as both will come in handy if you are writing your own.

1. JOB APPLICATION

Although varied in specific form, job applications contain several customary questions. Most applications ask for certain character references, which usually means former employers. In the case of a first job, naming teachers or high school counselors is acceptable.

Most employers will contact a reference if one is provided, so notify the person that he or she may receive a phone call from the prospective employer.

2. THE JOB INTERVIEW

Contrary to the premonitions of most students, job interviews are not the most stressful part of the process. When an employer asks to interview a potential employee, it generally means that the applicant has a chance of being hired.

Remember to project your best side at these meetings. There is no use in accentuating the negative sides of your character, unless the employer asks.

 Psst . . . Although it is better to overdress than underdress when interviewing, a sports jacket and slacks will suffice in almost any setting. Obviously, when applying for a house-painting job, lifeguarding, construction, McDonald's, and the like, your attire could be even less formal.

3. WRITING A RESUME

A polished resume becomes crucial in the adult world. Even in college, top-notch employers demand one. A resume should be typed or computer-generated, neat, and easy to follow.

Employers usually prefer short and to-the-point resumes. One page with all pertinent personal information should suffice; if your resume exceeds one page, cut out the least important material. A cover letter also should be included.

HOW DO YOU APPLY FOR WORK-STUDY JOBS?

Not everyone can get a work-study job, but anyone can apply.

The first step in applying, as with all other forms of financial aid, is to submit a standardized Financial Aid Form (FAF), obtainable from high school and college counseling offices. The College Scholarship Board then will inform applicants of the status of their application.

Once accepted into the work-study program, the student can choose from available positions and determine the times he or she wants to work. Because work-study usually serves as a form of financial aid, compensation for work may go directly to the university to cover tuition and housing. This depends on the specific program and the need of the student as determined by the board.

WAIT A SECOND! DO YOU EVEN WANT A JOB?

I chose not to work my first year at school, and I'm glad I didn't. For me, there were just too many things I wanted to do when I first arrived. Having a job would have taken a huge chunk of time out of a day with too few hours in it already.

During your freshman year, there are going to be so many new people you are going to want to meet. There are going to be hundreds of activities around campus that you should try out. Besides that, you have to account for studying—oh, and sleeping too. For me, I had to make time for the soccer team as well.

I don't know what I will do sophomore year. But, if you can help it, not working during your freshman year is definitely something to think about.

—HEIDI WIEDEMANN, DUKE UNIVERSITY

Many students feel working at school is too big a sacrifice. Before committing to any job, no matter how wonderful it may be, remember that school should come first . . . that's usually what you are trying to pay for anyway.

Despite this cautionary note, realize that many successful students have found it perfectly possible and even enjoyable to work and study simultaneously.

Sample Cover Letter

November 23, 1992

Barney Rubbish
Bedrock University
P.O. Box 12345
Bedrock, Maine 98765
(456) 867-5309

Mr. Wayne Bruce
BAT CAVE ACCESSORIES
10001 Batcave Avenue, Suite 13
Gotham City, North Dakota 01928

Dear Mr. Bruce:

I am interested in the internship your company offers college undergraduates who are pursuing a career in cave carving.

Presently, I am a freshman at Bedrock College where I plan to major in geology. As you can see from the enclosed resume, I have had experience working as a rock cutter for Fred Flinstein Rock Cutting on a part-time basis. I am considering cave carving as a long-range career possibility.

Please send me all relevant information with regard to the internship.

Thank you for your time, and I look forward to speaking with you again.

Sincerely,

Barney Rubbish

Sample Resume

Barney Rubbish

Present Address:
Bedrock University
P.O. Box 12345
Bedrock, Maine 98765
(456) 867-5309

Permanent Address:
1111 11th Avenue SE
Big Apple, New York 20212
(212) 456-7890

OBJECTIVE: To obtain a position as a rock cutter with a corporate firm.

EDUCATION:

9/89–present
Bedrock University, Bedrock, Maine. Course work includes: Geology, rock cutting, earth science and dinosaur training. Major: Geology. GPA – 4.0

8/85–6/89
Big Apple High School, Big Apple, N.Y. G.P.A. – 4.0

WORK EXPERIENCE:

6/91–present
Dinosaur Trainer, Bedrock Museum, Bedrock, Maine. Trained dinosaurs to do dog tricks at Bedrock Museum.

6/90–9/91
Assistant Rock Cutter, Fred Flinstein Rock Cutting, Bedrock, Maine.

HONORS/AWARDS:
Wilma Flinstein Science Award
Dean's List, Bedrock University
Member of Dinosaur Bone Collecting Club

SKILLS:
Word processing, computer graphics

FOREIGN LANGUAGE:
Spanish, Sanskrit

REFERENCES:
Jack N. DeBeanstock
Giant Beanstocks, Inc.
133 121st Avenue
Metropolis, New York 20213
(212) 867-2233

CHAPTER 25

Commuting

> *I graduated early from high school — right after junior year. At 17, the thought of living away from home seemed overwhelming and scary. Besides, I wasn't really into the big "party scene" that seemed to go along with campus life.*
>
> —KIRA LEHNER, HOFSTRA UNIVERSITY

> *My university doesn't have any dorms, so there wasn't a whole lot of choice about commuting. However, I did know that I wanted to live away from home, so I opted for off-campus housing. St. John's has advertisements for nearby apartments posted in Marillac Hall, so I just kept checking until I found one that was right for me. To me, it was the best of both worlds: being able to commute to school and still having the independence of being out on my own.*
>
> —SUSAN BOLSTER, ST. JOHN'S UNIVERSITY

Not everybody lives at school. In fact, if you are not considering commuting your freshman year, you probably will at some point during your college career.

There are several advantages to commuting. Some students can find cheaper housing away from campus. Others prefer living outside the campus environment, whether it be with a few friends in an apartment in a nearby city or with their parents in the comforts of home. Some need to work and have a job which is not located near their college. Regardless of your reasons for commuting, here are some tips to keep in mind.

SET YOUR ALARM CLOCK

If you're a commuter, set your alarm clock and leave early. Students who live on campus don't have to deal with bus schedules, traffic, and/or finding a parking spot. You do! And sometimes that's not such an easy task.

> *Probably the worst thing about commuting to USC was the traffic. I never knew how bad it was going to be. Sometimes it took me an hour to get to school, other times only 15 minutes. I ended up always leaving an hour early and bringing extra work in case I had some time before class.*
>
> —SHANNON STRASSER, UNIVERSITY OF SOUTHERN CALIFORNIA

Psst ... At most colleges, students who commute by car have to apply and pay for parking privileges. Find out about parking before you start school. Finding vacant spots on campus or on side streets is often difficult and can be dangerous, especially in questionable neighborhoods.

PICK THE RIGHT SCHEDULE

This is especially important for commuters. Avoid scheduling your first class at 9:00 and your second at 1:30. Although some commuters may be able to go home in the lapse, many will not. Passing four or five hours on campus can be rough when you don't have a dorm room or anywhere to unwind.

> *For several semesters I managed to get all my classes on Tuesdays and Thursdays (taking an evening class if necessary). Besides the luxury of going to school two days a week, I had the time to get a much-needed part-time job.*
>
> —ERIC HAFKER, QUEENS COLLEGE

TRY TO STAY IN TOUCH WITH CAMPUS LIFE

As a commuter, I was nervous that I would never meet any other students or have any connection with USC. So, I made a concerted effort to try to meet people in my classes. To my surprise, it was pretty easy. I met two other commuters on the first day. Both of them were feeling the same way I did. Now we meet for lunch on campus about two times a week. I feel a lot more comfortable walking around campus knowing that I have a few good friends.

—SHANNON STRASSER, UNIVERSITY OF SOUTHERN CALIFORNIA

It's common to feel lost or out-of-touch your freshman year, especially if you attend a large college. For commuters, who lack the opportunity of socializing in the dorms or Greek houses, assimilating can be an even tougher challenge. Here are a few tips to help you cure the commuter blues.

1. DON'T GO HOME AS SOON AS CLASSES ARE OVER.

If you have free time after class, take a walk around campus and visit the student center. Most student centers will have a bulletin board with job listings, summer internships, and local sports and social opportunities. Your college may also have a commuter club which sponsors social events specifically for commuters.

2. SET UP A CARPOOL.

Carpooling is an excellent way to meet other commuters. Most schools will have listings of other students living in your area who want to carpool — check with your school's parking administration office, commuter club, or student center. As an added bonus, many schools will actually reduce your parking fee if you join a carpool.

3. SET UP DATES WITH PEOPLE YOU MEET ON CAMPUS.

One way to force yourself to get involved in the campus community is to set up dates with other students you meet in class or on campus. Plan to meet someone for lunch in your school's cafeteria or deli. Study over a cup of coffee at a local cafe. Remember that you are not alone. Most students — commuters especially — will welcome the chance to get to know a new person on campus.

4. TAKE ADVANTAGE OF YOUR SCHOOL'S OFFERINGS.

College will afford you hundreds of opportunities that you may never have again. Before you leave, make sure you attend at least one campus play, art show, music performance, or sports event. Use the library and computer resources. Attend a lecture in a subject that sounds interesting. Just because you're a commuter doesn't mean that you have to miss out completely on your "college experience."

> *The toughest thing for me about being a commuter was breaking out of my shell. I remember spending a lot of my free time freshman year studying in the library or just going home early. It was tough to hang around school when you didn't know anyone.*
>
> *Gradually I began to realize that little things could make a big difference, like eating in the cafeteria when I was by myself, hanging out in the student center, and studying outside on the benches instead of cooped up in the library. Running into classmates and getting familiar with the campus helped me to open up, make more friends, and get more involved in activities.*
>
> —CHRISTINA BUFFAMONTE, HOFSTRA UNIVERSITY

Epilogue

College provides a cushioned entrance to the real world. While you don't have to pay taxes or hold down a full-time job, you still will be learning basic survival skills, the ones detailed in previous chapters. Indeed, college is your first step toward real independence.

The road to graduation is not always straight; there will be peaks, valleys, and curves. But if you set some goals, keep your chin up, maintain a sense of humor, and have fun in the process, college truly can be "four of the best years of your life."

 Psst . . . In the tritest of terms, I hope you had as much fun reading this book as I did writing it. And if you learned something in the process, that's even better. I know I did.

Greg Gottesman

AUTHOR

GREG GOTTESMAN
School: Stanford University
Major: Political Science
Hobbies: Tennis, journalism, government, writing college books
Piece of Advice: "Be yourself, unless no one else can stand you."

CARTOONIST

STEVE OJEMANN
School: University of Washington
Major: Political Science/Biology
Hobbies: Waterskiing, drawing, philosophy
Piece of Advice: "A very popular error: having the courage of one's convictions; rather it is a matter of having the courage for an attack on one's convictions."
—Friedrich Nietzsche

CONTRIBUTORS

RICO ALEXANDER
School: Stanford University
Major: Biology/Pre-med
Hobbies: Volleyball, tennis, basketball, Nintendo
Piece of Advice: "Free your mind, and your ass will follow."
—George Clinton

RICK ARNEY
School: Stanford University
Major: Economics/Political Science
Hobbies: Going to A's games, driving, writing, badminton
Piece of Advice: "Don't forget your parents."

CHRISTINA BUFFAMONTE
School: Hofstra University
Major: Publishing Studies & Literature
Hobbies: Drawing, reading, writing, music
Piece of Advice: "Have fun experimenting with a wide variety of courses — not just the ones related to your major."

PADDY CARSON

School: University of Colorado at Boulder

Major: Broadcast production management

Hobbies: Skiing, life

Piece of Advice: "There's so much more to college than academics, but in order to experience more, you have to stay in school."

BRYAN COHEN

School: Claremont McKenna College

Major: History/Government

Hobbies: Music, nudity, fish, drama, government

Piece of Advice: "Don't take life so seriously, or you will implode."

MATT CRILE

School: University of Washington

Major: International business

Hobbies: Rugby, reading, guitar

Piece of Advice: "Don't ever change to suit someone else."

LESLIE FRIEND

School: University of Chicago

Major: Music

Hobbies: Playing the cello, tennis

Piece of Advice: "Work as hard as you play, and play as hard as you work."

ANDY GOTTESMAN

School: University of Michigan

Major: Political Science/ Communication

Hobbies: Writing, reading, baseball

Piece of Advice: "College is sharing Oreos and hot chocolate with friends after a Michigan victory on a crisp, sunny football Saturday."

JESSICA HALL

School: Syracuse University

Major: Magazine Journalism

Hobbies: Writing, photography

Piece of Advice: "Resist the urge to count down the days until winter or spring break. Ninety-seven days and counting will only depress you."

TARA McCANN

School: Stanford University

Major: Political Science/ Communication

Hobbies: Piano, dance, movies, parasailing

Piece of Advice: "The majority of my college education didn't come from text books and lectures but from 3 a.m. discussions with friends and heated debates with the guy down the hall."

THOM McDADE

School: Pomona College

Major: Biosocial Anthropology

Hobbies: Skiing, backpacking, river rafting

Piece of Advice: "Get involved at your school whether it be athletics, academic clubs, or social awareness groups. Play an active role in the community. It's a great way to make friends."

WHITNEY B. MORRIS

School: Pomona College

Major: Government

Hobbies: Dance, skiing, rugby

Piece of Advice: "Studying isn't enough. Join organizations and groups that interest you. Become involved in your college community."

TAMI OSTROFF

School: Pomona College

Major: Anthropology

Hobbies: Dance, watching sports, hanging out

Piece of Advice: "Be open-minded and don't have specific expectations."

JAMIE REYNOLDS

School: Stanford University

Major: English/Latin American Studies

Hobbies: Basketball, theater (technical), singing, foreign beer connoisseur

Piece of Advice: "Relax and take it easy. Let college adapt to your pace. Remember you're the one who's paying."

STANLEY RYTER

School: University of Washington

Major: Civil Engineering

Hobbies: Skiing, basketball, hiking, traveling, government

Piece of Advice: "If at first you don't succeed, ask her out again."

JOHN GERARD SCHREUDER

School: University of Washington

Major: Bioengineering

Hobbies: Sports, photography, travel

Piece of Advice: "Don't waste your college years by taking school too seriously."

DAVID STERN

School: Cornell University

Major: Government/English

Hobbies: Cycling, tennis, reading

Piece of Advice: "Take a year off to do something other than go to school for four years—spend a year abroad, work, travel."

KEITH VERNON

School: University of Puget Sound

Major: Business/Finance

Hobbies: Money, tennis, skiing, people

Piece of Advice: "If you exert yourself 100 percent, you can never be disappointed with your results."

NOELEEN WALDER

School: Stanford University

Major: Psychology/Visual Anthropology

Hobbies: Photography, reading, writing, stressing out

Piece of Advice: "Don't stress out about a major. Try a lot of different areas before you settle down into one."

MARTINA STEWART

School: Yale University

Major: English and African-American Studies

Hobbies: Moviebuffery, figure skating, aerobics (step, slide, and funk)

Piece of Advice: "You've gotta live on the edge. Otherwise, you're just taking up space."